GUIDE TO LEGAL WRITING STYLE

ASPEN PUBLISHERS

GUIDE TO LEGAL WRITING STYLE

FOURTH EDITION

TERRI LeCLERCQ
Senior Lecturer and Fellow,
Norman Black Professorship
in Ethical Communication in Law
University of Texas School of Law

Wolters Kluwer
Law & Business

AUSTIN   BOSTON   CHICAGO   NEW YORK   THE NETHERLANDS

Aspen Publishers
Attn: Permissions Department
76 Ninth Avenue, 7th Floor
New York, NY 10011-5201

To contact Customer Care, e-mail customer.care@aspenpublishers.com, call 1-800-234-1660, fax 1-800-901-9075, or mail correspondence to:

Aspen Publishers
Attn: Order Department
PO Box 990
Frederick, MD 21705

Printed in the United States of America.

1 2 3 4 5 6 7 8 9 0

ISBN 978-0-7355-6837-2

Library of Congress Cataloging-in-Publication Data

LeClercq, Terri, 1946-
    Guide to legal writing style / Terri LeClercq. – 4th ed.
        p. cm.
    Includes index.
    ISBN 978-0-7355-6837-2
    1. Legal composition. 2. Law—United States—Language. I. Title.
KF250.L3913 2007
808'.06634—dc22   2007016254

About Wolters Kluwer Law & Business

Wolters Kluwer Law & Business is a leading provider of research information and workflow solutions in key specialty areas. The strengths of the individual brands of Aspen Publishers, CCH, Kluwer Law International and Loislaw are aligned within Wolters Kluwer Law & Business to provide comprehensive, in-depth solutions and expert-authored content for the legal, professional and education markets.

CCH was founded in 1913 and has served more than four generations of business professionals and their clients. The CCH products in the Wolters Kluwer Law & Business group are highly regarded electronic and print resources for legal, securities, antitrust and trade regulation, government contracting, banking, pension, payroll, employment and labor, and health-care reimbursement and compliance professionals.

Aspen Publishers is a leading information provider for attorneys, business professionals and law students. Written by preeminent authorities, Aspen products offer analytical and practical information in a range of specialty practice areas from securities law and intellectual property to mergers and acquisitions and pension/benefits. Aspen's trusted legal education resources provide professors and students with high-quality, up-to-date and effective resources for successful instruction and study in all areas of the law.

Kluwer Law International supplies the global business community with comprehensive English-language international legal information. Legal practitioners, corporate counsel and business executives around the world rely on the Kluwer Law International journals, loose-leafs, books and electronic products for authoritative information in many areas of international legal practice.

Loislaw is a premier provider of digitized legal content to small law firm practitioners of various specializations. Loislaw provides attorneys with the ability to quickly and efficiently find the necessary legal information they need, when and where they need it, by facilitating access to primary law as well as state-specific law, records, forms and treatises.

Wolters Kluwer Law & Business, a unit of Wolters Kluwer, is headquartered in New York and Riverwoods, Illinois. Wolters Kluwer is a leading multinational publisher and information services company.

Dedication

Maj. Donald Lee Miller, 1923-2003

This book was written to supplement the teaching of legal writing faculty who have such enormous jobs: If law students will work through these pages and apply these style principles to their drafts, the faculty will be free to concentrate on analysis; on effective feedback; and on student progress.

Mary Hendryx, my diligent assistant, helped me prepare this manuscript, and here I get to say "Thank you!" Beth Youngdale, who has taught students throughout Texas in statewide Pre-Law Institutes, also taught me much about analysis and helped me develop the organizational chart in Chapter 2. Excellent law librarian Jeanne Price helped me untangle Bluebook and ALWD rules (but any errors are my own). Many editors have helped proofread this manuscript, including Carole Wood.

I remain grateful for the personal and loving support of my husband, Jack Getman.

SUMMARY OF CONTENTS

CONTENTS

MESSAGE TO STUDENTS

So here you are in law school, and it's back to learning how to write.

WHY STUDY WRITING — AGAIN?

No matter what academic and life experiences you've already had, you will immediately realize that legal writing is different. It's a skill, and, like any new skill, it has to be practiced.

Yes, it's still writing, but it is a **branch** of technical writing with its own set of rules and priorities. Although you learned to write in grade school, composed essays and organized reports in high school, and perhaps created analytic discussions in college or on the job, there's more! Each of those writing stages helped you reach the next stage — and the next stage. Now you've reached a narrowed branch within the field of technical writing. You'll discover that legal writing reflects the very skill you learn in your law classes: spotting the legal issue and comparing/contrasting that to other cases and policies.

When you begin writing legal documents for class, your first draft will follow the outline your legal faculty provides or your legal-writing text suggests. Formulaic? Yes. So was learning the five-paragraph essay. Novice writers have to know the general skeleton required of them before they can leap off into a research paper; so, too, you need to practice the basic outlines for legal writing.

Legal writing is demanding in ways that undergraduate writing rarely is, perhaps because legal writing requires you to recognize both sides of any issue and simultaneously to be precise and concise.

WHY WASTE TIME ON WRITING SKILLS?
(Didn't I come here to learn torts?)

It's not easy to meet the new demands of law school; new terminology, excessive daily readings, and complicated abstractions create insecurity in even the most confident students. It is natural, then, to focus on learning the information in torts and contracts classes. That alone takes more time than anyone has, and yet there's a legal-writing skills class, too.

Unlike many torts and contracts classes, your legal-writing class can offer concrete feedback about organizing, analyzing, and applying facts. Unfortunately, many students try to circumvent the very process that will help them learn doctrine: that of analyzing cases and organizing their thoughts toward a better understanding of the law. Other law students give it the old undergraduate sideswipe and hope it suffices until they have time to really concentrate on writing.

Those reactions are mistakes — costly mistakes.

Practicing legal writing is practicing the law. Learning to be concise is learning to focus on the essential issue and cut extraneous arguments. Learning to find the precise case precedent and precise word is learning to analyze in your argument. That's what law school is about, and it's how writing fits into the practice of law. Visualize an audience of hurried, irritated, and probably bored readers. (Does this describe your first-year study group as well?) You must convince them that you have something they need to read and that you have thoroughly analyzed each side's position.

Your memorandum or brief or letter is not the most important part of your readers' day; it's only part of their job:

- They are not reading it uninterrupted.
- They are not reading it during mental prime time.
- They are not interested in the law for law's sake.
- They do not expect to be entertained or amused.

Somehow, you have to get them to read, and to act on, your ideas or conclusions. That's your job.

In undergraduate school, it's the professor's job to read student writing. A student's job was to turn in his or her best work (although most of us can remember turning in a "draft" as a final paper and getting away with it). When graduates leave and start their professional roles, though, they have to fulfill the professional expectations of their audiences — just as soon as they guess who the audience is and what that new audience expects.

IF LEGAL WRITING IS SO IMPORTANT, WHY ARE MY CASEBOOKS FULL OF CONVOLUTED OPINIONS?
(Is someone kidding?)

Not many readers can defend the prose of judicial opinions selected for casebooks, a style students instinctively assume is "the way law looks." We can't defend this prose because it is so very terrible — you're right. Perhaps you can get some perspective if you realize that

- the case was probably written years ago when writers used a more lofty, elevated language,
- casebook authors include cases not for their prose style but for the issues they present, and
- there are a lot of bad writers in the legal profession — but don't join them!

Remember your frustration when you read your casebooks — you don't want your readers to respond that way to your own prose.

HOW CAN I MAKE BEST USE OF THIS BOOK?

This book is meant to be a purely practical guide to your new readers' expectations. The book is divided into six parts that can help you break down the task of editing your drafts into credible final products. First review the basic rules of professional writing by trying the five exercises in Chapter 1. Once you're assured that you remember the rules required for professional writing, then skim this book before beginning your first assignment; you'll see what is important in that new field. Then allow this checklist to keep you on track:

CHECKLIST for ORGANIZATION, Chapter 2:

- Did I conscientiously shift from undergraduate to legal organization?
- Did I experiment with an outline in the margin of my draft?
- Can readers easily find both the conclusion and setup at the beginning?
- Do my headings and topic sentences reflect the order of the setup?
- Can readers follow the coherent whole through my use of carefully chosen transitions?

CHECKLIST for SENTENCES, Chapter 3:

- How long is too long for each of my sentences?
- Have I placed my verb close to its subject?
- Is the main clause obscured by an initial dependent clause?
- Are modifiers close to the noun they modify?
- Are parallel ideas represented by parallel structure?
- Did I review each sentence and revise unnecessary passive voice?
- Are long quotations absolutely necessary, or can I paraphrase them?

CHECKLIST for WORDS, Chapter 4:

- Have I inadvertently included legal jargon?
- Did I spend time deleting unnecessary words?
- Did I edit from the concluding sentence to the first, examining pronouns for their proper antecedents?
- Are the strings of nouns and adjectives properly hyphenated to indicate noun strings, or can I break up the string?
- Did I edit to replace nominalizations?
- Did I review my list of frequently misused words?

CHECKLIST for PUNCTUATION, Chapter 5:

- Do my punctuation marks help the reader understand the substantive material, pulling words together and apart appropriately?
- Have I reviewed the general punctuation list?
- Have I double-checked those marks required specifically for legal writers?
- Do those marks conform to Bluebook/ALWD style?

CHECKLIST for FORMAT, Chapter 6

- Is my document visually inviting?
- Is the organization readily apparent?
- Can readers understand what's important through my use of white space and paragraph/sentence length?
- Have I added the final visual touches of proximity, alignment, repetition, and contrast?

This book cannot answer all of your style questions or calm all of your anxieties. But if you use it as a springboard for constant and deliberate practice, you'll develop into a careful legal writer.

April 2007

Terri LeClercq

GUIDE TO LEGAL WRITING STYLE

Just as novice legal readers can be confused by the distinction between holdings and dicta, so too can novice writers misunderstand the difference between grammar rules and stylistic suggestions.

Terri LeClercq, Expert Legal Writing 177 (1995)

✦ ✦ ✦ ✦

1

REVIEWING
THE BASICS

There is little sense in polishing your legal style if your underlying control of basic English rules destroys your credibility. Following is a series of short tests that will help pinpoint any grammar, punctuation, or word choice problems you may still need to review and correct. Answers to the first set of questions appear right below the respective examples so that you can quickly evaluate yourself. Answers to the second set appear immediately after the list of questions. The answers to the last three sets are tucked away in the Appendix at the back of the book, along with answers from the other chapters. So that the short tests are challenging, some of the examples may be correct.

After this review, you can always slip in the accompanying CD and continue practicing on errors you have discovered through these first short exercises.

FIVE BASIC REVIEWS

BASIC REVIEW # 1

1. Once the prison doors closed, Ed decided to lay down in his cell to think.
to **lie** down
lay = put or place
lay/laid/laid
lie = recline
lie/lay/lain

2. Covering his head with the small blanket, his eyes were still blasted by the overhead light.
When **he covered** his eyes with a small blanket, **he** was still ... *or* ... blanket, **he could** still sense the blast of the overhead light.   Dangling element.

3. He first tried to block out thoughts of whomever had lied in his trial.
whoever had lied.   Subject of clause (who had lied) dominates placement as object of preposition.

4. Rather, he focused on pulling the virtual covers up and to think of the coming three years.
and thinking.   Parallel structures (on pulling) and (on thinking).

5. Neither the blinding light nor the intimidating guard would be as depressing as his trial had been.
Correct

6. He thought of the number of days in three years but he had a hard time imagining how many days that really was.
years, but he.   Punctuation between two independent clauses.

7. The relatives and friends that he would miss would move on with their lives.
whom he would.   People require animate pronoun, things receive inanimate "that."

8. Perhaps he would find alot of acquaintances here who could take their places for this time.
a lot.   Two words, always two words!

9. He thought a bit about his food and wondered if they would be as horrible as he had heard.

if **the food**, or if **the cooks**.   Ambiguous pronoun.

10. Ed dreaming of food was not unusual.

Ed's dreaming or **Dreaming of food, Ed** was not . . .   Possessive before a gerund.

Did you score 100%? If not, continue practicing with the next sets of reviews. Plus you can learn Ed's lessons while you're at it.

BASIC REVIEW # 2

1. Ed's door automatically opened to the clang of a shrill bell, and Ed's buildings occupants quickly filed out.
2. The line seemed comprised of men who looked exactly like he looked.
3. Most looked resigned, unhappy or habitually angry.
4. Naturally, Ed had arrived expecting this.
5. Mostly he hoped he was not the most unique new prisoner in the line.
6. He was only hoping to fade into the blur of faded shirts and pants.
7. A nearby new prisoner and Ed's fears were quite different.
8. Each of the experienced prisoners had their eyes on both men.
9. Ed finally picked up his serving tray the man behind him dropped his with a clatter.
10. The server behind the line gave the tray-dropper the smallest of the two portions.

Answers to Basic Review #2

1. Ed's **building's** occupants.   Possessive even after another possessive.
2. **composed of**. The building comprised many men.   Incorrect word.
3. resigned, **unhappy,** or habitually.   Punctuation in a series.
4. expecting **these expressions**.   Ambiguous "this" requires concrete noun.
5. **was not unique** in the line.   The word "unique" cannot be qualified.
6. **hoping only to fade**.   Misplaced modifier.

7. **prisoner's** and Ed's. Different fears, so each must be possessive with plural noun.
8. had **his** eyes. The word "each" is singular and traditionally requires a singular pronoun.
9. **tray. T**he man or **tray; t**he man. Two independent clauses require terminal punctuation.
10. **smaller.** Comparative with two; superlative (smallest) with three or more.

BASIC REVIEW # 3. See Answers, pp. 97–98.

1. Thus Ed began his lessons in how the prison hierarchy develops.
2. They sat at a long table with fifty four legged metal chairs.
3. A man across asked the two, "Are you new here"?
4. Since they had not been at the table at breakfast, Ed presumed the man already knew the answer to that question.
5. Barely no time passed before the other prisoner responded and offered his name.
6. Keeping his eyes on his plate, he tried to chew quickly, and hoped no one would assume the two new prisoners were together.
7. When he had finished gulping his food and waiting for the next stage of his first prison day Ed kept his eyes on his plate.
8. The lunch period ended with it's stylized three-bell cacophony.
9. A prisoner has: no privacy and little communication while inside his cell.
10. It was concluded by Ed that these years were going to be very, very long and boring.

BASIC REVIEW # 4. See Answers, p. 98.

1. Everyone from new prisoners to 20-year inhabitants were determined to research their legal options.
2. Research in the prison library was different than any investigation he had made before.
3. A sign on the library wall quoted a U.S. District judge, who was unhappy with a filing, as saying "Your pleadings are so argumentative that it is easy for the defense to deny everything, including the periods and commas".

4

4. Since he was a poor writer, Ed was afraid to begin his request for a re-hearing.
5. The librarian who had been a paralegal in his earlier life explained that there is no actual set of laws that Ed could read that applied directly to his trial.
6. Recognizing his common dismay, the librarian produced a well-worn summary of trial errors.
7. Hopefully, this list pinpoints Ed's major issues.
8. He only needed to find whether his lawyer could sleep through witness testimony.
9. Hidden in all the small-type books had to be a specific law, which he needed to argue his case.
10. Another prisoner thought Ed could imply the court's response to his petition by reading the huge file of old petitions.

BASIC REVIEW # 5. See answers, pp. 98–99.

1. Ed fantasized that someone had summarized specific criminal law for his fellow inmates and he.
2. After weeks of sitting in the hard metal chairs he asked the librarian if there was a file of previous cases that had helped prisoners with ineffective counsel cases.
3. When the experienced librarian heard the tension in Ed's voice, he suggested that Ed slow down; Ed replied that he had slown down for weeks and actually wanted to research faster instead.
4. Reluctantly the librarian opened the locked desk drawer, and removed an envelope of yellowed newspaper articles.
5. There was a year-old case on top, which had a prominent headline about a man given a re-trial because his lawyer had slept through much of the testimony.
6. Attempting to control his anger, Ed wondered why the librarian had not shown the article to other prisoners and himself sooner.
7. The librarian had been a paralegal and knew something about the law, however, he was afraid to offer legal advice and be held accountable to any of the prisoners he would continue to see daily.

5

8. The newspaper article referred to the Model Code of Professional Responsibility, Canon 6 — "A lawyer shall not . . . neglect a legal matter entrusted to him."
9. The Model Code of Professional Responsibility requires each lawyer to represent clients "with zeal" to insure a just outcome.
10. Picking up his blank yellow notepad, Ed began creating his petition for rehearing before the court that had sentenced him to prison while his lawyer slept.

Only as we tumble our words onto the page or into a dictating machine do we begin to see our story, our argument, take shape. The time to focus on the relationships between the disparate parts of our document is during the reading of the first draft. Only then can we see that point one is independent of point two, but that points three and four are inexorably tied to the outcome of point two and thus dependent.

TERRI LECLERCQ, EXPERT LEGAL WRITING 60 (1995)

2

ORGANIZING WITH STYLE

An undergraduate paper and a legal memorandum or brief share many elements of good writing. Still, legal readers have been trained to expect a specific order of information, so this chapter helps you adjust to those expectations. This new organization is at first frustrating, so you might have one of at least two responses: (1) you can bang your head on the desk and insist to your professor that he simply doesn't understand your brilliant analysis, or (2) you can read the chapters in your legal-analysis text and also this chapter, take a deep breath, and follow the formula. Remind yourself that you have come to law school to learn and that this different organization, however it is presented in your analysis text, is one of the first important lessons of law school.

UNDERGRADUATE VERSUS LAW SCHOOL ORGANIZATION

Legal organization differs from general undergraduate organization in several important ways: you will find it more formulaic, more repetitive, and more dependent on sources than on flashes of insight. The chart below highlights the organization differences:

Undergraduate Papers	Legal Memoranda
GOALS **Deductively move from big picture with specific examples** • prove research • show spark of imagination or innovation • general resolution/recommendation	**GOALS** **Inductively synthesize elements of cases** • answer specific legal question • apply Rule (statute/cases) to client's facts • address both sides of the issue • conclude with likely outcome
INTRODUCTION • general **history** or background of topic • **thesis** usually last sentence	**INTRODUCTION** • brief **conclusion** • restate **Rule** to be examined • **road map** of following discussion • client's **facts**
STRUCTURE • follows **thesis** • needs **topic sentences** to support thesis • needs **transitions** to connect major sections, sentences	**STRUCTURE** variation of IRAC but will always include • the **Rule**; • aspect of, or all of, the **Issue;** • an explanation that describes the pertinent **cases** that have analyzed the Rule; • an **Application** that compares and contrasts the cases' facts with the current client's facts; • **Counter-analysis** that anticipates what the other side will see differently; and • a **Conclusion** for each point

SUPPORTING AUTHORITY	SUPPORTING AUTHORITY
• **primary material** (First Amendment, below, or two paintings of Washington on the Delaware, etc.) • **outside authority** (journal articles, Web materials, interviews, etc.)	• **relevant cases,** always includes name of case, court, jurisdiction, year • may occasionally allow for secondary sources such as law reviews, restatements
CONCLUSION • **brief repetition** of contents of paper and conclusion • a **general resolution** to problem/issue raised • perhaps a spark of imagination or innovative suggestion	**CONCLUSION** • restatement of **overall conclusion** from various points made • perhaps list of facts to be discovered • perhaps suggestion for next step in legal process

Below is an undergraduate paper with its elements labeled on the left in familiar terminology. To the right is the new terminology you will apply to those same elements, plus terminology for the new and different elements of legal writing. As you will quickly realize, an undergraduate paper and a legal memorandum share many elements of good writing.

	SCHOOL PRAYER TODAY	
Essay "title" will ▶ reflect its contents.		▶ "**MEMO**" (or a court filing)
Background ▶ covers topic.	Throughout the past few decades, prayer in public schools has been a major social issue that has moved into the federal courts' arena. The First Amendment to the Constitution states that "Congress shall make no law respecting an establishment of religion, or prohibiting the free exercise thereof." The court focus lately has been on prayer, over a loudspeaker, at a public football game. After examining both sides of the argument, I will explain why the best solution is a moment of silence before any sporting event.	▶ Here, **specific facts** of a client's case would lead to the **Issue.** (Our client would like to lead a prayer at his son's local school's football game.) ▶ Also the **Rule** (First Amendment language) and major/recent cases that interpreted the **Rule.** ▶ Then a **road map** would anticipate the organization.
Thesis anticipates ▶ organization ("both sides") and conclusion ("best solution").		
Topic sentence ▶ **Flowing** ▶ **structure**	Many American citizens believe public prayer is a Constitutional right and should not be restricted. They point to the "no . . . prohibiting the free	▶ **Topic sentence**, with a brief **Conclusion**, will introduce one prong or cases

9

Authority for ▶
support can be
from almost
anywhere.

No pressure to ▶
see which court or
if opinion still
valid law.

exercise" language. Nearly 70% of evangelicals believe that the public school system does not allow students enough religious freedom (Christianity Today, Nov. 2006), and an even larger percentage of Christians is generally in favor of prayer during sporting events. They argue that non-religious participants and fans should feel no pressure to join these prayers because the noise, excitement, and crowd movement allow individual privacy (unlike a quiet classroom setting). Who leads the prayer is also important: a player, a teacher, or a religious leader. "The burden is on the viewer" to tolerate or ignore inoffensive speech," said the 1975 court in Erznoznik v. City of Jackson.

that analyze the
Rule and **Apply**
cases' facts and
holdings.

▶ Support will
come primarily
from **case
language** and full
citation.

▶ Then those facts
will be **com-
pared** and
contrasted to the
client's.

▶ **Counter-
argument** is
required, plus
this point's
conclusion.

Topic sentence ▶

Outside authority ▶
for support

Legal authority ▶
for support

No support for ▶
statistic

Newspaper ▶
authority

Many American citizens believe public prayer is a Constitutional right and should not be restricted. They point to the "no . . . prohibiting the free exercise" language. Nearly 70% of evangelicals believe that the public school system does not allow students enough religious freedom. (Christianity Today, Nov. 2006), and an even larger percentage of Christians is generally in favor of prayer during sporting events. They argue that non-religious participants and fans should feel no pressure to join these prayers because the noise, excitement, and crowd movement allow individual privacy (unlike a quiet classroom). Who leads the prayer is also important: a player, a teacher, or a religious leader. "The burden is on the viewer to tolerate or ignore inoffensive speech," concluded the 1975 court in Erznoznik v. City of Jackson.

▶ **Topic sentence,**
with a brief
conclusion, will
examine the
second prong of
issue or case.

▶ Facts from
case(s) are
applied to
client's facts.

▶ Finally, **conclu-
sion** of second
prong or case.

Conclusion ▶
repeats the thesis.

**Shows spark of ▶
innovation.**

Considering the wide diversity and strong feelings about prayer at sporting events, a compromise is necessary: a moment of silence. That way, those who believe that the government shouldn't restrict their right to commune with

▶ **Overall Conclu-
sion** unites all the
issues, perhaps
with a mention of
disputed facts to
be investigated
and perhaps with
a suggestion of

> their god should have their moment to do so. And those who observe the silence can also fantasize about their team's victory or whatever comes to mind in the din around them. The non-religious could thus allow room for the religious without intruding on or restricting others. Those who fear a Trojan horse forcing prayer on the non-religious should remember the court's admonition that "the burden is on the viewer."

where to go from this point.

After your law professor hands you a hypothetical with specific facts, your job will be to first see if you can "issue spot" from those facts. Writers naturally produce a hash of ideas, marginalia, and cases. **It's a draft**.

Now, how do you get from a draft to a final product that must lead readers through the writer's ideas and legal precedent behind those ideas? Some writers, naturally organized, begin with an outline that they fill in as the research develops. Others flail around, scribbling and drawing arrows until they understand what it is they're writing about. Whatever a writer's preliminary organizational strategy, readers will have to follow the resulting progression of ideas. That's why, as a writer, you need to reserve time beyond what's required for the initial researching and scribbling. Unlike some of the undergraduate assignments all of us turned in, legal assignments always require a revision, a fresh eye, to decide how best to help readers find what they need. Deciding on your macro and micro organization should be your first step.

Look back at that first essay and the marginalia for legal writing. Its macro (overall) organization includes a general introduction, an indication of the order and cohesion of major points (the setup), and your conclusion. The micro (paragraph) level is your paragraph development and internal cohesion. If you give readers a strong introduction and follow it logically, readers can skim the introduction and headings and quickly know both what the document is about and how the parts fit together.

ORGANIZING YOUR RESEARCH: MARGIN OUTLINES

A useful technique for evaluating what you've uncovered through research and drafting is to type out your ideas as you've scribbled them, putting them into whatever order seems best for the moment. That can mean typing case summaries first, or your list of policy considerations, etc. Just get them down. (Don't throw away your notes, because you'll undoubtedly need them later.) Print them out and see what you've got.

In the margin of that draft copy, jot one word or phrase that summarizes each paragraph's main point. Then quickly read through your marginalia, checking to see if they follow a logical order. If they do, decide whether that order fulfills your audience's needs. If not, you can rearrange with a massive cut-and-paste. Sometimes you'll be able to delete whole paragraphs of repeated material.

A major obstacle that novice legal writers must overcome is the temptation to organize case by case. You need to practice legal thought, and thus writing, as a progression of issues (not cases). Then you support those issues with authority, the cases.

INTRODUCTION: THESIS AND ROAD MAP

After moving your draft sections into a logical order, you need to create an introduction (which may be the first paragraph, or several) that includes

- A **thesis** announcing your major point or conclusion and
- A **road map** announcing your organization.

This internal cueing anticipates the major point(s) and divisions of your argument, which allows readers to feel comfortable with what follows. A comfortable reader is a grateful reader.

The introductory paragraphs explain your main **thesis** (usually your conclusion) in the context of the overall issue. Some legal readers expect to find the conclusion attached to specific facts; others don't. If the overall thesis depends on several legal points, you should begin each section with a small-scale version of the introductory thesis and road map.

In addition to the thesis, you will create a **road map**, which is a textual outline of the information to follow. The road map lets readers know in advance the relative *weight* of the parts and the *order* in which they will be discussed.

Thesis statements vary by function: the thesis of a *memorandum*, for example, is predictive, leading the reader from the legal issue to a short, general conclusion that is afterward supported by a balanced, analytic survey of pertinent theories and cases. In contrast, the thesis of a *brief* is persuasive rather than predictive, and thus announces a conclusion supported through cases and policy.

A **road map** foreshadows the organizational pattern to follow. It might, for instance, be a quick overview of three exceptions to a general rule. Or it might be a list of theories that you will examine. Like a literal road map, it lets travelers (your readers) know how long they will be on the road, what they will find the most interesting, and which minor roads to expect along the way.

USING HEADINGS AS SIGNPOSTS

Long documents *require* headings; shorter documents are *aided* by them. In either case, your readers will benefit from the quick overview of the larger picture in your thesis and setup, and can then skim your headings. As a writer, you will also benefit when you take time to summarize the paragraphs' contents as headings: if the headings in your first draft don't summarize your discussion when you skim them, or if the headings bounce you around from one idea to another, you are now on alert to make the necessary adjustments to your draft.

Guidelines for Headings

A bonus for careful writers is the visual effect of headings: Readers can be pulled by the headings and subheadings to the section of specific interest.

1. Headings need to **satisfy the readers' needs**. Headings labeled "Element One," "Element Two," and "Element Three" do not satisfy anything. Instead, a heading should summarize the material within that block of text.

2. Headings should **reflect the setup.** If you insert a major heading to introduce one element of negligence but do not use headings for the following two, your reader won't understand that those three elements are parallel.

3. Headings can consist of single words, phrases, or sentences, but they should **be consistent in content, grammatical structure, and typography.** If the first major heading is a full sentence, then all the other major headings should be full sentences. Similarly, the subheadings may be only phrases, but then each subheading should be a phrase. If major subheadings are flush left and in bold face, then sub-subheadings need to be differentiated as a group by a consistent indent, or they should be in italics.

4. Headings should be **independent of the text** that follows them. The following portion of a brief relies on its heading for its logic; if readers skipped the heading, they would find themselves in the middle of a fact discussion that has no legal context. The writer has left the context back up in the heading and has forgotten to reestablish it within the textual discussion.

X   Attorneys Cannot Use Pleading to Harass

Powe believed that his motion on behalf of the teacher was backed by strong evidence that she had been discriminated against by her administration. He had no knowledge of a Fourth Circuit requirement that a client must go through collective bargaining as a member of a school district. Thus, he counseled her not to ask for collective bargaining before the filing.

USEFULNESS OF TOPIC SENTENCES AND TRANSITIONS

Topic sentences work in much the same way as a thesis: they introduce the idea within the paragraph; they set boundaries for the paragraph; and they help tie ideas together. Reexamine the previous student essay, noticing that each paragraph from a carefully constructed undergraduate paper contained a topic sentence that introduced or summarized the paragraph's content.

Experiment with your own rough drafts by separating each topic sentence from your text: is each one a strong introduction to, or conclusion about, that paragraph's main idea? Next, examine the coherence of the topic sentences as they relate to the overall setup. At this point, you may decide that some added transitions will smooth the reader's path.

Examine the undergraduate paper again, this time for its transitions, and where you might have added them if this were your draft. The idea that transitions are important is a strange one, and yet they perform a critical function in connecting ideas. Whether connecting large-scale segments, paragraphs, sentences, or words, transitions signal relationships.

1. Traditional transitions explain those relationships right up front: *again, once, first, finally, however.* As the writer, it is your job to connect words and ideas so that your readers don't have to do the mental work for you. Your legal readers should be able to trace how you structure your discussions, descriptions, and arguments by focusing on these transitions. Some writers worry that they cannot begin a sentence with "however." Wrong. It creates the juxtaposition with whatever word or phrase follows it.

Powe believed that his motion on behalf of the teacher was backed by strong evidence that she had been discriminated against by her administration. *However*, the Fourth Circuit required that a client must go through collective bargaining as a member of a school district.

Powe believed that his motion on behalf of the teacher was backed by strong evidence that she had been discriminated against by her administration. The Fourth Circuit, *however*, required that a client must go through collective bargaining as a member of a school district.

2. Repetition of words/ideas can create cohesion, as can **dovetailing** (using words with a similar linguistic base like "deny" and "denial"[1]).

Gerardi will have **two arguments**. **First**, he will **argue** that the case he relied on was only recently overturned, and thus the law in that area could be considered **unsettled**. Where a particular area of law is **unsettled**, an attorney will not be held liable for failing to know it. **Morrill v. Graham**, 27 Tex. 646, 652 (1864). **In Morrill**, an attorney failed to **present** a claim against a decedent's estate within the proper time period. Whether the **presentment** was required, the Texas Supreme Court ruled, was an "open and controverted point, **so** the attorney was not negligent in failing to present the claim." Morrill, 27 Tex. at 652. **This first argument** cannot be successful, **though**, because the court further stated that law is **settled** once it has been **"settled by the adjudications** of our courts." Morrill, 27 Tex. at 652. The legal issue was **adjudicated** when the Texas Supreme Court issued a decision on the point, thus **settling** the law according to the Morrill court's definition.

Second, Gerardi may argue that because the decision he failed to discover was relatively recent, he should **therefore** not be required to find it. He is correct that Morrill mentions, as one factor in determining attorney liability, the "difficulty, nay, often the absolute **impossibility of access** by attorneys to the ordinary sources of information" that prevailed at that time. Morrill, 27 Tex. at 652. Morrill was decided in **1864. From 1864 to 2007**, however, communication technology and the proliferation of law libraries have significantly improved the **possibilities of access** to ordinary sources of information by any

---

[1] See, for instance, the detailed discussions of dovetailing in OATES & ENQUIST, THE LEGAL WRITING HANDBOOK 608-12 (4th ed., Aspen Publishers 2006).

> attorney. **Therefore**, in response to Gerardi's **second argument**, the court will more likely find that knowledge of a six-month-old case is well within an attorney's duty.

3. Case names and citation information are not topic sentences nor transitions. When readers begin a paragraph without an effective topic sentence, they cannot assimilate a new case name and citation into your textual flow. See Chapter 3, p. 40–42.

EXAMINING YOUR ORGANIZATION

There is no right or wrong way to organize; effective organization is determined by both the audience and the message. Focusing specifically on organization, however, will help you review your thought process and logic as you develop thesis, road map, headings, topic sentences, and transitions.

Here's a useful tip for examining the organization of your draft: cut the draft into paragraph blocks, scramble the blocks, and reassemble them to their original order using only the topic sentences and transitions. If you have to reread the full contents of each of your own paragraphs to recognize their content, imagine how difficult it would be for your reader to follow what you are saying! Better return to the draft and sharpen your internal cues.

If you want to tighten your document even more, cut one of your paragraphs into separate sentences, mix-up the sentences, and ask a friend to reorganize the paragraph. If your friend can't find the topic sentence and reassemble the original, return to that draft. You're not finished.

What to Remember

Here's a logical sequence for that second run-through of your scribbled research:

- **Summarize** each paragraph in the left-hand **margin.**
- **Cut/paste** paragraphs into the organization your audience will expect.
- **Move** into your front paragraphs information an audience needs to understand your conclusion.
- **Create** a **road map** anticipating your organization.
- **Add headings** that follow your setup and act as signposts.
- **Create topic sentences** that anticipate each paragraph's content.
- **Add transitions** to connect major sections and paragraphs.
- **Conclude** with a reminder of the setup or add a summary of additional information needed.

CONCLUDING EXERCISES: **ORGANIZATION**

See Answers, pp. 99–103.

ALSO REVIEW EXERCISES ON ACCOMPANYING **CD.**

1. Organization. Evaluate how this appellate opinion might be organized after this setup. Can you envision alternatives?

Discussion

The McPhails contend that Louisiana should recognize automobiles as dangerous instrumentalities and hold commercial owners/renters liable when their vehicles are negligently operated. They claim that public policy considerations support their contention. Rentacar argues that Louisiana should not adopt the dangerous instrumentality theory in the context of automobile liability. They point to other states that have rejected the theory.

2. Thesis and road maps. Many readers would not be able to follow the road map paragraph below. What is the problem with the headings or road map, and how would you correct it?

Rule 11 of the Federal Rules of Civil Procedure requires attorneys to certify that any pleading or written motion is filed not to harass, or to delay, and to certify that the claims and contentions are not frivolous. In the instant case, Powe believed that his motion on behalf of the teacher was backed by strong evidence that she had been discriminated against by her administration. He had no knowledge of a Fourth Circuit requirement that a client must go through collective bargaining as a member of a school district. Thus, he counseled her not to ask for collective bargaining before the filing.

3. Headings. Develop the headings that might follow the paragraph above or that might follow your own, improved paragraph.

4. Road map paragraphs and headings. Are the headings anticipated? Are they effective divisions for the road map?

Powe's evidence probably proves that his motion on behalf of the teacher was not frivolous. Generally, federal courts are lenient about accepting evidence that an attorney is not filing merely to waste time. The Fourth Circuit, however, has established precedent that collective bargaining is required before a complaint can be filed in court. Several other circuits have discussed but not applied this requirement.

a. The General Rule and the Fourth Circuit's Requirement
b. Case Law
c. Counter-Analysis

5. Headings. Quickly skim only the introductory paragraph. Next, evaluate the *headings* that follow. Are these headings a reasonable follow-up to the introductory paragraph, and if not, what should they be?

If the measure for malpractice is the "reasonably competent practitioner standard," clients will not be able to overcome the great burden of proving their attorneys acted unreasonably. Frank Cosgrove sustained injuries as the result of an automobile accident. After the expiration of the limitations period, Mr. Cosgrove discovered that his attorney, Walter Grimes, had filed suit against the wrong person and alleged the wrong location. Mr. Cosgrove wants to file a malpractice action against his attorney alleging negligence, breach of contract, false representations, and Deceptive Trade Practices Act (DTPA) violations. The court will probably hold that the first two charges fall within the "reasonably competent" standard but will reject the DTPA charge.

a. The court investigated the "subjective good faith" excuse and found that there was no excuse for attorney negligence.
b. His attorney had stated that he had indeed filed the lawsuit, when in fact he had left the task to another attorney and failed to ensure the filing.
c. The court would not award mental anguish damages for the false representation or DTPA claims.

6. Headings. Next, read the paragraph below and create your own headings that would logically follow this introductory paragraph.

An appellate lawyer must consistently serve his/her client by mastering the record, thoroughly researching the law, and exercising judgment in identifying arguments that may be advanced on appeal. Yolanda Denise Walder used court-appointed counsel to file a brief in which her counsel argued that the State failed to prove that Walder's failure to pay her (earlier) fine and to do her community service was intentional, and that the trial court denied her right to counsel by denying her a continuance. The brief cited one case, one statute, and one constitutional provision as support. The appellate court determined Walder's brief was deficient because it did not provide adequate citations to pertinent legal authority. The Sixth Amendment requires appellate counsel to render effective assistance on behalf of his/her clients. Case law has interpreted the amendment to cover thorough research of the law. Quite simply, the Rule of Appellate Procedure 38.1 provides clear guidelines for the form of a brief.

a. _____

b. _____

c. _____

7. Headings. Evaluate this heading and its supporting first paragraph.

• • • • • • • •

C.   The Oregon Supreme Court, in the recent In re Gatti, 8 P.3d 966 (Or. 2000), sanctioned a lawyer who misrepresented his identity while attempting to investigate a claim of insurance fraud.

> Thus, the Oregon court refused to recognize "an exception for any lawyer to engage in dishonesty." 8 P.3d at 976. Not all states adopt as strict an approach. New York, for example, has long recognized prosecutorial exceptions to the dishonesty rule.

8. Transition. Add transitions and delete unnecessary language to help readers follow this discussion.

The plaintiff argues that a determination should be made under Federal Rules of Evidence 194(a) (inadmissible evidence may be considered). The defendant argues that Rule 104(b) controls (only admissible evidence may be considered). The court agrees with the plaintiff. The court notes that determinations under Federal Rules of Evidence 104(b) must be based on admissible evidence. The courts note that Rule 104(b) applies only to determinations of "the relevancy of evidence." Determining whether a document is a business record does not involve the document's relevancy. The court concludes that Rule 104(b) does not apply. The court concludes that the determination of whether a document is within Rule 803(6) should be made by the court under Rule 104(a). In no known instance has this been a matter for a jury to decide. The Third Circuit agreed with this reasoning in <u>In re Japanese Electronics Products</u>, 723 F.2d 238, 287-88 (3d Cir. 1983).

9. Topic sentences and transitions. Rewrite the following draft paragraph so that readers can anticipate its contents and follow its reasoning.

In <u>Walder</u>, the court ruled that counsel must serve a client to the best of his or her ability. <u>Walder v. Texas</u>, 85 S.W.3d 824, 829 (Tex. 2002). There, counsel did not identify the appropriate standard for appellate review of a revocation order. In <u>Cosgrove</u>, the Texas Supreme Court ruled that counsel had a duty to act as a reasonably prudent professional. There, counsel did not recognize the statute of limitations in a car accident that occurred in another state. <u>Cosgrove v. Grimes</u>, 774 S.W.2d 662 (Tex. 1989). The holdings of these cases were similar. Both courts held that attorneys have a duty of reasonable care to serve their clients. In Mr. Gerardi's case, the issue presented is whether overlooking a major development in case law is reasonable.

10. Transitions. Review this memorandum's statement of facts. Reorder sentences, delete unnecessary details, and add or change transitions to create coherence.

Pamela Hunter filed suit on behalf of a group of bakery workers. She filed a class-action suit in North Carolina. The workers believed that their bakery had violated Title VII of the Civil Rights Act of 1964 when the bakery closed. Ms. Hunter argued that the bakery had a pattern and practice of racial discrimination. Compared to the predominately white workers at other company-owned bakeries, the predominately African-American workers in this bakery were more skilled but paid less. The owners had publicly stated that this store would remain open throughout the year.

The bakery denied the allegations. The bakery insisted that any Title VII claims had to be arbitrated under a collective bargaining agreement (CBA). The bakery asked the court to impose a Rule 11 sanction on Hunter for filing a lawsuit when she knew or should have known of the CBA. The North Carolina court sanctioned her and suspended her legal practice for five years.

Five other circuits have held that Title VII claims do not have to be first arbitrated under a CBA.

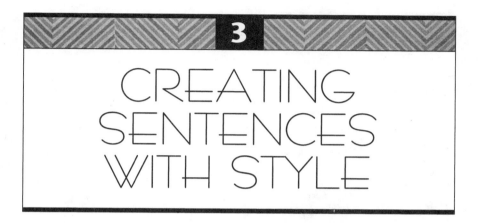

CREATING SENTENCES WITH STYLE

It's back to your original draft for a look at readability: will your readers understand everything on a first read-through, or are your sentences so long and convoluted that your readers will be forced either to reread or to abandon all hope?

Predictably and sadly, it takes most new law students about a week before they begin producing sentences that resemble those in casebooks. Giving in to this subliminal seduction is natural, but it is also counterproductive for novices trying to express new legal concepts on the written page.

This chapter examines problems that commonly affect the readability of sentence-level legal prose. One technique for reviewing your draft is to look at the individual sentences and ask: Who Did What to Whom? Discounting the "to be" verbals, you can edit many weak sentences into powerful ones by adding the actor into sentences that originally were passive, for instance, or moving a citation out of the subject slot so that a specific court "held" or "concluded." The idea behind this review of sentence structure is that you'll return to your now-organized draft and tackle each sentence until it says specifically and concretely what you want it to say. That requires time — the same sort of time your future legal documents will demand.

Unraveling tough sentences

- Long sentences
- Subject/verb separation
- Front-loaded sentences
- Missing signposts
- Passive/active voices

See Exercise 1

Avoiding error

- Treacherous and misplaced words
- Faulty parallelism
- Pronoun/antecedent placement

See Exercise 2

Incorporating authority

- Awkward citation placement
- Excessive/intrusive quotations

UNRAVELING TOUGH SENTENCES

Most legal sentences are too long and too convoluted for easy reading. You will find copious examples the first time you open any casebook to a random page. Those long sentences are the result of legal training, which, as you are learning, is a process of qualifying, narrowing, and delineating with evidence. Thus your new skill at qualifying and delineating while you are "thinking like a lawyer" can inadvertently result in a chain of clauses that becomes long, convoluted, written sentences.

One frustrating and "tough" aspect of legal sentences is their unending dependent clauses, formulated first perhaps in the classroom when you attempt to answer a professor's pounding questions. You qualify simple, declarative sentences with independent, qualifying phrases. That helps with classroom answers, certainly. But who ever heard of an important case holding that expressed itself in a subordinate clause?

Not all long sentences are difficult reading, of course; no set number of words or typed lines breaks readability rules. If legal sentences are carefully punctuated and cued, then necessary qualifications will not affect the document's readability. Without proper cueing, though, a chain of embedded, dependent clauses will confuse readers:

> **✗** In an unpublished 2000 Sixth Circuit case from Tennessee, the court, distinguishing as many as 30 counts against professors and students at the University of Tennessee Space Institute (UTSI), some of whom worked for a private atmospheric research firm that had contracts with NASA and the Department of Defense, and one, the evidence proved, plagiarized at least 92% of one dissertation from materials supplied by his professor, who was also the president of the private firm, and another who was given credit for a thesis that was 95% identical to the first student, had to decide if there was fraud and by whom.

SOLUTIONS

1. Where possible, **break long sentences** by separating embedded clauses into separate sentences.

   a. Break into two or more sentences.

   In an unpublished 2000 Sixth Circuit case from Tennessee, the court had to decide if there was fraud and by whom. **The court distinguished** as many as 30 counts against professors and students at the University of Tennessee Space Institute (UTSI), some of whom worked for a private atmospheric research firm that had contracts with NASA and the Department of Defense.

One student, the evidence proved, plagiarized at least 92% of one dissertation from materials supplied by his professor, who was also the president of the private firm, and another ~~who~~ was given credit for a thesis that was 95% identical to that of the first student.

b. Break into two sentences **plus** add a transition.

In an unpublished 2000 Sixth Circuit case from Tennessee, the court had to decide if there was fraud and by whom. The court distinguished as many as 30 counts against professors and students at the University of Tennessee Space Institute (UTSI), some of whom worked for a private atmospheric research firm that had contracts with NASA and the Department of Defense. **For instance,** several counts were based on evidence that proved that one student plagiarized at least 92% of one dissertation from materials supplied by his professor, who was also the president of the private firm, and another ~~who~~ was given credit for a thesis that was 95% identical to that of the first student.

In an unpublished 2000 Sixth Circuit case from Tennessee, the court had to decide if there was fraud and by whom. **First,** the court distinguished as many as 30 counts against professors and students at the University of Tennessee Space Institute (UTSI), some of whom worked for a private atmospheric research firm that had contracts with NASA and the Department of Defense. **Then, the court looked at** evidence that proved one student plagiarized at least 92% of one dissertation from materials supplied by his professor, who was also the president of the private firm, and another ~~who~~ was given credit for a thesis that was 95% identical to that of the first student.

2. Place the **subject close to the verb** and place both of them toward the beginning of the sentence.

X The **Department of Defense and the Department of the Army,** which had employed many of the faculty and potential Ph.D. candidates and paid them for both their credentials and their work product, **charged** the defendants with scheming to defraud the United States of money or property, in violation of the Mail Fraud Act.

The **Department of Defense and the Department of the Army had employed** many of the faculty and potential Ph.D. candidates and paid them for both their credentials and their work product. **They charged** the defendants with scheming to defraud the United States of money or property, in violation of the Mail Fraud Act.

3. **Identify front-loaded sentences**. Your readers will not be able to grasp the point of each sentence when long, or complicated qualifying, or descriptive information *precedes* the main subject. They can't hold all that introductory language in abeyance until the main noun shows up.

✗ Convicted of each of the 31 counts except for obstructing justice but convinced that their conduct was within the range of acceptable for academic studies and simultaneous outside work, the **defendants**, who filed separately and collectively in several different courts on their series of convictions, **brought** appeals based on the scheme to fraudulently provide degrees from UTSI in exchange for student efforts to funnel government contracts.

This sentence places 29 words *before* the beginning of the main clause — and the main subject (the defendants) is then *separated* by 14 more words from the sentence's active verb (brought). Try the techniques below to sharpen your prose: make sure the main subjects of your sentences appear near the beginning where the reader expects them — either break the sentence into two or flip-flop it so that the main subject appears in its natural, and expected, position at the front.

a. **Break up** a front-loaded sentence into two sentences.

The **defendants had been convicted** of each of the 31 counts except for obstructing justice but **were convinced** that their conduct was within the range of acceptable for academic studies and simultaneous outside work. Therefore, the **defendants brought** appeals separately and collectively, in several different courts, arguing that they did not have a scheme to fraudulently provide degrees from UTSI in exchange for student efforts to funnel government contracts. (shorter, readable)

b. Flip-flop the sentence so that the main subject and verb are first.

The **defendants brought appeals**, separately and collectively, in several different courts on their series of convictions that were based on the scheme to fraudulently provide degrees from UTSI in exchange for student efforts to funnel government contracts because, though they had been convicted of each of the 31 counts except for obstructing justice, they were convinced that their conduct was within the range of acceptable for academic studies and simultaneous outside work. (much longer, and certainly less readable)

A bit of strategy: You may deliberately create a front-loaded sentence if you need to hide its true message.

4. **Missing signposts** cause reader confusion, so **add word and punctuation signposts** if the sentence length is absolutely necessary.

   a. Careful **word signposting** can help defeat necessarily long sentences by signaling relationships: transitions, repetitions of words or phrases, introductions, and conclusions. (See Chapter 2, p. 15).

   The court **first** held that the convictions were based on insufficient evidence to support the "degrees for contracts convictions" **and thus** dismissed ten counts **but then** remanded to the district court for a hearing as to whether one plaintiff should receive a new trial on the basis of a *Brady* conviction.

b. In addition to word signposts, **punctuation signposts** can make the message more accessible, as the following colon illustrates:

On appeal, all defendants argued that the prosecutor had violated the *Brady* rule: defense counsel should have been provided a copy of the report from Department of the Army criminal investigators.

c. Finally, you can also use **numbered lists (tabulation)** to create an organizational hierarchy (and add white space to the page).

✗ Defendant Potter argues that she should be granted relief from misjoinder because she was unfairly prejudiced by the evidence presented against the other defendants, the denial of these motions was reversible error, the prosecution was guilty of abuse of discretion, the testimony at trial relating the "the degrees for contracts" theory had a prejudicial spillover effect under Rule 14, and the issue is not barred by res judicata.

Defendant Price argues that
1. she should be granted relief from misjoinder because she was unfairly prejudiced by the evidence presented against the other defendants,
2. the denial of these motions was reversible error,
3. the prosecution was guilty of abuse of discretion,
4. the testimony at trial relating the "the degrees for contracts" theory had a prejudicial spillover effect under Rule 14, and
5. the issue is not barred by res judicata.

Thus, as you sharpen your draft, you can use transitions and dovetailing, punctuation, and tabulation to help your readers understand necessarily long sentences.

5. Replace **passive voice** with active, generally. We've all been taught to avoid the passive voice, but a rare few of us remember what it is. A quick review: a verb is "active" when the subject of the sentence is performing the action: "The **court held** that the defendant was negligent." But if the subject is acted upon by something else (as this very clause demonstrates), the verb is passive. *The plaintiff was injured by the vehicle.* Don't confuse the passive voice with the past tense: *The attorney had defended and prosecuted the same man.* Overuse or inadvertent use of the passive voice causes several problems:

a. Adds unnecessary words.

 The term "cosmic detachment" **is used by** Richard Wydick to explain abstract legal style. (14 words)

Richard Wydick **describes** abstract legal style as "cosmic detachment." (9 words)

b. Steals the punch from strong, active verbs.

 The University was injured by this unusual, nonacademic scheme.

This unusual, nonacademic **scheme defrauded** (cheated, stole the integrity of) the University.

c. Introduces ambiguity: truncated passives (person/agent missing).

 No **rebuttal was made** about the reputation of future Ph.D. degrees. (who might have rebutted?)

The Ph.D. **candidates** who had turned in plagiarized dissertations **did not rebut** diminution of future Ph.D. degrees.

d. Misplaces emphasis.

 The dissertations **were turned in** to faculty who also worked for the outside research firm. (who turned them in?)

These Ph.D. **candidates turned in** their plagiarized dissertations to faculty who also worked for the outside research firm. (candidates . . . turned in)

On the other hand, the passive voice is useful when used deliberately:

■ when you *do not know* the agent/actor.

The girl was propelled out of the train.

■ when you need to *protect* your "subject" from a direct accusation.

Marta was dismissed from law school.

■ when you want to *emphasize the result* of an action.

George was murdered by a drunken driver.

Try These

EXERCISE 1. UNRAVELING TOUGH SENTENCES. See answers, p. 103.

Either (1) justify leaving the following sentences at their current length or (2) create a more understandable sentence by breaking phrases into separate sentences; punctuating or dovetailing them for clarity; repositioning subject and verb; or tabulating.

1. The district court, noting that the report was *Brady* material because the report did identify the fraud procurement advisor as a favorable witness, and that the advisor might have testified that the government did not suffer any economic loss when the scholars plagiarized, concluded that the material should have been disclosed.

2. On those factual grounds, the court concluded that the report does contain exculpatory material, the government failed to respond to the defendant's specific requests for the material, and there is a reasonable probability that testimony from Kennedy could have influenced the trial so the report should, therefore, have been disclosed by the government as *Brady* material.

Experiment with flip-flopping and then breaking apart these front-loaded sentences. Which of your rewrites reads more smoothly?

3. Because a roommate of one of the Ph.D. students discussed the issue with her own advisor and that faculty member had been worried about government funding of academic projects, the advisor felt morally bound to report the questionable behavior to the university's honor committee.

4. If the prosecution suppresses requested evidence favorable to an accused when the evidence is material either to guilt or punishment, irrespective of the good or bad faith of the prosecution, the suppression violates due process.

Switch the following passive constructions into the active voice.

5. A nationally syndicated columnist was plagiarized in a law student newsletter by a third-year student.

6. He was uncovered by the Federalist Society.

7. It was later learned that the column was meant to be edited before publication.

AVOIDING ERRORS

Treacherous placement of a word or phrase can have serious consequences. It is unfortunately easy to *inadvertently toss* onto a page something that pops into your mind. In the same way, serious consequences develop in legal writing if a *word can modify more than one antecedent* (its "head word"), if it modifies the *wrong antecedent*, and also if words *aren't placed exactly* where they need to be. Finally, if parallel ideas aren't written in *parallel constructions*, then readers misunderstand the intent of the sentence.

SOLUTIONS FOR ERRORS

1. Place modifiers precisely—**directly before or directly after** the word or word groups they modify.

 I have placed a newspaper ad for an honest lawyer and paralegal.

As written, the respondent to the ad must definitely be an honest lawyer; the writer **may also** require that the paralegal be honest. Daily, courts are forced to interpret contract clauses with modifiers floating among several nouns.[1] Look at the reader's dilemma created below by a tiny, limiting modifier (almost, only, even, just). Each solution might be correct, depending on the writer's intent:

He shot himself in the foot Monday.
Only **he** shot himself in the foot Monday.
He *only* **shot** himself in the foot Monday.
He shot *only* **himself** in the foot Monday.
He shot himself *only* **in the foot** Monday.
He shot himself in the foot *only* **Monday**.
He shot himself in the foot Monday *only*.

2. Evaluate each modifier that might be interpreted to **modify more than one** noun.

---

[1] For examples of treacherous placement of words that have been litigated and required court interpretation, see TERRI LECLERCQ, Doctrine of the Last Antecedent, 2 J. OF LEGAL WRITING INST. (1996) 81.

X The candidate must pass the written test and the durability test within one week before beginning work. (**must** take durability test within a week; **might** also have to take written test within a week — but it's ambiguous)

a. Add comma.

The candidate must pass the written test and the durability test, within one week before beginning work. (must do both within one week)

b. Move to modify full clause.

Within one week of beginning work, the candidate must pass the written test and the durability test. (must do both within one week)

c. Break into two sentences.

The candidate must, within one week before beginning work, pass the written test. He also must pass the durability test.

d. Separate antecedents and add "also," etc.

The candidate must pass the written test within one week before beginning work, and he should also pass the durability test.

3. Beware of **multiple pronoun antecedents.**

Because he was screaming abuses, the defendant ordered the police officer to arrest the man. (Who was screaming: The defendant? The police officer? The man? We need the pronoun attached to or replaced by one of the nouns for clarity.)

4. Dangling elements may cause faulty antecedents; that is, the noun being described by a clause isn't even in the sentence. Grammarians refer to these constructions as "dangling elements" because a reader can't connect the phrase with anything explicitly inside the words of the sentence:

> ✗ Reading multiple books a day, the library was always my favorite relaxation spot.

Because **I** read multiple books a day, the library was always my favorite relaxation spot.

Reading multiple books a day, **I** always sat in the library, my favorite relaxation spot.

5. Be specific with **relative** and **demonstrative** pronouns.

Demonstrative Pronouns	Relative Pronouns
this	who, whom
that	that, which
these	what, whatever
	whomever, whoever
	whichever

> ✗ The Model Code of Responsibility says a lawyer may not "threaten to present criminal charges solely to obtain an advantage in a civil matter." DR 7-105. **This** would focus lawyers for both sides on the actual issue.

The Model Code of Responsibility says a lawyer may not "threaten to present criminal charges solely to obtain an advantage in a civil matter." DR 7-105. **This limitation** (*or* restriction) would focus lawyers for both sides on the actual issue.

> ✗ A lawyer may not "threaten to present criminal charges solely to obtain an advantage in a civil matter," **which** keeps lawyers on both sides focused on the issue.

A lawyer may not "threaten to present criminal charges solely to obtain an advantage in a civil matter," a **limitation that** keeps (*or* "a civil matter that keeps") lawyers on both sides focused on the issue.

6. Keep **syntactically equal** items parallel.

> **X** Koby's interaction with the Human Rights Commission included **creating an inventory** of past issues and **assistance** with current European cases.

Koby's interaction with the Human Rights Commission included **creating an inventory** of past issues and **assisting with** current European cases.

7. Review your **numbered lists,** which highlight grammatically parallel items.

> **X** Other provisions of Section 6 provide (1) **for** the requisites of the application for a bondsman's license, (2) **for** an investigation and hearing by the board, and (3) **its denial** of the application or approval conditioned on the applicant's filing of the required security deposit.

Other provisions of Section 6 provide (1) **for** the requisites of the application for a bondsman's license, (2) **for** an investigation and hearing by the board, and (3) **for** its denial of the application or approval conditioned on the applicant's filing of the required security deposit.

8. Keep **signals** parallel to reflect parallel ideas and parallel structures. Some writers have trouble with a list and its introductory word or phrase that they later *repeat*. Or, on the flip-side, writers might lose that parallel because a signal is *missing* that would pinpoint which items are parallel.

   a. Repeated introductory word.

36

✗ The dishonesty rule represents poor policy, is open to constitutional challenge, and it violates due process. ("it" repeats the introductory noun "rule")

The dishonesty rule represents poor policy, is open to constitutional challenge, and violates due process.

b. Missing signal for parallel list.

✗ The state bar committee has helped the image of attorneys by not allowing dishonest attorneys to practice, publicizing pro bono activities, and educating members of the bar about professional conduct. (because one item is in the negative, writer should repeat the introductory *by* to create the parallel)

The state bar committee has helped the image of attorneys by not allowing dishonest attorneys to practice, by publicizing pro bono activities, and by educating members of the bar about professional conduct.

✗ Thus, the court held that the complaint was not vague or conclusory and it was "adequate to give notice of the claims asserted."

Thus, the court held **that** the complaint was not vague or conclusory and **that** it was "adequate to give notice of the claims asserted."

9. Keep items parallel that follow **correlative conjunctions**.

either . . . or
neither . . . nor
both . . . and
not only . . . but also
whether . . . or

The Ph.D. students plagiarized material **not only** from their major professor's research **but also** from government documents labeled "classified."

X **Not only** were the first-year students afraid of the new professors **but also** their classmates. (emphasizes *were the first-year students*)

The freshman students were afraid **not only** of the new professors **but also** of their classmates.

10. Avoid losing parallelism with **an inadvertent repetition** of "that" in a string of clauses.

X The plagiarists said **that** because the government had an inspector whose files were not turned over **that** the appeal was a *Brady* appeal.

The plagiarists said **that,** because the government had an inspector whose files were not turned over, the appeal was a *Brady* appeal.

Try These

EXERCISE 2. AVOIDING ERRORS. See answers p. 104.

Examine the placement of modifiers in these sentences. If they are misplaced or ambiguous, correct them. If they represent two or more interpretations, be prepared to explain those possibilities.

1. One student tried at least twice to notify the Dean, who was titular head of all graduate students, who she thought would understand her situation.

2. After researching both primary and secondary sources, you must turn in a draft and have it read and edited within two weeks of graduation.

3. This court only reversed the convictions for "degrees for contracts" but allowed the defendants to renew their Rule 14 claims in district court.

Rewrite the following sentences, replacing ambiguous pronouns and limiting the antecedent that a pronoun can refer to.

4. The court questioned whether the government investigation included information material to the plaintiffs' facts and if this would thus establish a legitimate *Brady* claim.

5. The plaintiffs had their understanding of the material and the government kept some of the material from the plaintiff's lawyer, so it was up to the court to review it.

6. Ph.D. candidates are expected to do their own research and write their own original papers. Newspapers wrote a series of articles about them.

7. Detective Miller's counsel did not cross-examine the student in the presence of the jury and now contends, as he did on direct appeal, that by not being able to go into the student's background, he was prevented from showing his bias or prejudice for testifying as he did, in violation of his Sixth Amendment right to confrontation.

Redo these sentences as necessary to create parallel items within them.

8. Within a graduate department, the faculty is always divided over how many graduate students one faculty member can supervise simultaneously and teaching large classes without appropriate help from teaching assistants.

9. In defense of dissertation, a student must present:

   a. an oral defense of the topic's thesis;
   b. that the thesis is original and not a repetition of another's earlier work;
   c. a bibliography of works consulted; and
   d. supervisors' work with drafts and alternative hypotheses.

10. A Ph.D. candidate must ask his chairman for direction, sources, personal library holding, and give him or her the draft early enough for feedback.

INCORPORATING AUTHORITY

Legal writing is characterized by its need for, and excessive use of, authority. This tension is first a surprise and then a constant challenge to legal writers. Intruding citations and long, direct quotations create stumbling blocks for readers. Citations are necessary, important, and generally compact; still, they can intrude on your sentence's meaning. Of course citations are important to document legal points. Do not, though, let their location in your sentences obscure your substantive message.

A second common writing problem for those who read legal documents is a long quotation that disrupts the textual discussion with **no introduction**. If the writer were to briefly introduce the quotation, perhaps using a sentence that gives the gist of the material following, then readers would have a context before reading and might even understand where their attention should be.

SOLUTIONS

1. Awkward citation placement.

   a. Move citations into prepositional phrases.

✗ *Office of Disciplinary Counsel v. Surrick,* 750 A.2d 441 (Pa. 2007), maintained that the plagiarism charges should apply to the Ph.D. defendant.

A Pennsylvania court, in *Office of Disciplinary Counsel v. Surrick,* 750 A.2d 441 (Pa. 2007), agreed that the plagiarism charges should apply to the Ph.D. defendant.

b. Move citations to the end of your sentence.

The Pennsylvania court maintained that the plagiarism charges should apply to the Ph.D. defendant. *Office of Disciplinary Counsel v. Surrick,* 750 A.2d 441 (Pa. 2007).

c. Avoid ending one sentence with a citation and beginning the next sentence with another citation (back-to-back quotations).

✗ A Texas case allowed a university general counsel to determine the final plagiarism charge. *Student Ethics Committee v. Piddleheimer,* 150 S.W.3d 888 (Tex. 2007). *Office of Disciplinary Counsel v. Surrick,* 750 A.2d 441 (Pa. 2007), maintained that the plagiarism charges should apply to the Ph.D. defendant.

A Texas case allowed a university general counsel to determine the final plagiarism charge. *Student Ethics Committee v. Piddleheimer,* 150 S.W.3d 888 (Tex. 2007). **In the same year, a Pennsylvania court** became the final court, *Office of Disciplinary Counsel v. Surrick,* 750 A.2d 441 (Pa. 2007), maintaining there that the plagiarism charges should apply to the Ph.D. defendant.

d. Consider moving citations into **footnotes.** Citation footnotes return a legal document into the more familiar and readable form of an undergraduate paper, and some conditioned readers find it easy to drop their eyes down into footnotes to find which jurisdiction the case came from, or in which year the case was decided. If you are comfortable with your knowledge of your readers' preferences, then citation footnotes are an attractive solution to the traditionally citation-interrupted sentence. If you don't know your audience, and are unsure of their reading habits, sticking to *The Bluebook* and *ALWD Citation Manual* formula may be safer.

2. **Do not confuse** citation abbreviations with textual words. As the *ALWD Citation Manual* and *The Bluebook* explain, a citation used as a noun in a textual sentence is technically incorrect. The abbreviation is of course correct within a citation entry, but it is NOT correct as a noun within a sentence.[3]

 This case is governed by RPC 8.4(c).

Section 8 of the Rules of Professional Conduct governs this case. RPC 8.4(c).

3. Question the purpose of including each **long quotation**. Is all the language necessary to your particular point? Does all the language further your own analysis relating to your own fact pattern, or does some of that language take your reader out and into facts of the previous case? Too many long quotations are a signal of a hurriedly written discussion, a cut-and-paste job. One option is to quote only the essential element that distinguishes it from other authority. Then paraphrase the rest of the section. A second option is to keep that essential, on-point must-have long quotation but paraphrase everything else.

Compare the pros and cons of the following methods for incorporating text into your own discussion.

---

[3] *See* ALWD CITATION MANUAL R. 2.3 (3d ed. 2006); THE BLUEBOOK: A UNIFORM SYSTEM OF CITATION R. 10.2.1(c) (18th ed. 2005).

Long block quotations:

Pro	Con
add validity through stark presentation of language	are easily skipped by hurried readers
stand out on the page	can be difficult to integrate into a writer's textual point
can highlight extended controversial/ colorful language	can introduce extraneous material and even contradict the writer's intended point
	can create a black, dense look to a document
	can be interpreted as sloppy writing
	need an especially strong introductory tag line and conclusion in the writer's text
	reproduce poorly written prose of the original writer whose point is useful but whose prose is deadly

Shorter word/phrase quotations:

Pro	Con
integrate more easily into the writer's text	if used out of context, can destroy credibility
will keep the readers' focus on the writer's analysis rather than on case summaries	
allow a writer to retain colorful and controversial language that readers could find persuasive	

43

Paraphrasing:

Pro	Con
most successfully integrates outside information into a writer's own text	requires the writer to be more sophisticated with, and take more care to provide, careful signals
creates shorter, smoother documents	should not be used when the exact wording is in dispute
	can fail if signals indicating who/said/what are too weak for readers to follow
	can confuse readers if writer quotes more than one source within a sentence

After you've edited your draft's organization (with its thesis, road map, and headings), investigate your sentence-level prose: sentence length and order, passive and left-handed sentences, parallel structures, and placement of citations. As you read through your draft this time, review each sentence merely as a sentence — not as an information-carrier. This technique allows you to see your writing as your reader does: sentence by sentence. The time you expend tightening each sentence will eventually pay off by giving you credibility with your reader.

Try These

EXERCISE 3. INCORPORATING AUTHORITY. See answers, p. 105.

Move or correct the following citations using the above suggestions.

1. United States v. Frost, 125 F.3d 346 (6th Cir.1997), originally set forth the facts of the plagiarism case against the plaintiffs in this action.

2. After the Supreme Court decided, in <u>Brady v. Maryland,</u> 373 U.S. 83 (1963), that suppression by prosecutors of favorable evidence to the accused violates due process, <u>Kyles v. Whitley,</u> 514 U.S. 419 (1995), reviewed the materiality requirement and said a "touchstone of materiality is a reasonable probability of a different result."

3. 18 U.S.C. §1341, the Mail Fraud Act, prohibits people from scheming to defraud the United States of money or property.

What to Remember

- Review **sentence length,** keeping sentences as short as their meaning will allow.
- Place your **verbs close** to their subjects.
- Keep any initial **dependent clause short,** or move it behind the main clause.
- Review sentences to keep **modifiers close** to the noun they modify.
- Create **parallel** structure to highlight parallel ideas.
- Review each sentence and **revise** unnecessary **passive** voice.
- Keep only absolutely **necessary quotations** and paraphrase the others.

CONCLUDING EXERCISES: SENTENCES

See answers, p. 105.

ALSO REVIEW EXERCISES ON ACCOMPANYING CD.
First identify the stylistic error that each sentence represents. Then edit it for readability.

1. Owner and president of FIG, a private atmospheric research firm that relied primarily on contracts with government agencies including NASA and the Department of Defense, Defendant Bite was also a professor at the University of Tennessee Space Institute (UTSI).

2. It was decided by the plaintiffs to bifurcate both their claims and the individual cases so they could be heard separately and perhaps more fairly.

3. The students may have thought that as long as the supervising professor knew of and approved their use of outside materials that they were adequately documenting their material.

4. By presenting to the court a pleading, motion, or other paper, an attorney or unrepresented party is certifying to the best of the person's knowledge, information, and belief, formed after an inquiry reasonable under the circumstances, that it is not being presented for any improper purpose, and other legal contentions therein are warranted by existing law, and that the allegations and other factual contentions have evidentiary support or, if specifically so identified, are likely to have evidentiary support after a reasonable opportunity for further investigation or discovery, and that the denials of factual contentions are warranted on the evidence, or, if specifically so identified, are reasonably based on a lack of information or belief.

5. The grand jury returned thirty-one indictments against multiple defendants, charging them with scheming to defraud the United States of money or property and aiders and abettors in obstruction of justice.

6. Ph.D. students may only include material in their written work if they acknowledge the primary sources and keep the material exactly as it was originally.

7. In an unpublished opinion, the Sixth Circuit had complicated original facts and a tangled time line. <u>United States v. Potter,</u>

234 F.3d 1270 (6th Cir. 2000); <u>United States v. Frost</u>, 125 F.3d 346 (6th Cir. 1997), developed that set of facts in the earlier opinion, so the court could rely on their earlier decision for help through the lengthy list of names and causes.

8. Motions for acquittal were filed and a decision was rendered by the court only days later.

9. He had just faced his first interview with the hysterical adult daughter of a woman who'd been bludgeoned to death by her drunken husband.

10. Believing that unpleasant secrets from the ivory-tower university were to be revealed, the courtroom was packed with townspeople hoping to hear what makes academics so different from regular townspeople.

Cleansed of words without meaning, much of the language of the law need not be peculiar at all. And better for it.

DAVID MELLINKOFF, THE LANGUAGE OF THE LAW 454 (1963)

4
CHOOSING WORDS WITH STYLE

Once again, look at each sentence of your draft to ensure that it says exactly what you intended. It will come as no surprise that precise word choice can mean the difference between success and failure.[1] So, evaluating the words you have chosen, again repeat the mantra: Who Did What to Whom? Thus you will edit flabby draft sentences by replacing them with deliberate, strong nouns and strong verbs.

The list below pinpoints several categories of problematic words (ironically, the labels are English-teacher jargon, but I am hoping you recognize the list of terms before you read the more detailed explanations of the problems they cause).

- Jargon
- Wordiness

---

[1] Frisky students reading this chapter have suggested new titles: Choosing Words with Moxie, Flair, Pizzazz, Impudence. For your first assignment, I suggest you limit yourself to words with Style.

- Noun strings
- Nominalizations
- Treacherous and misplaced words

JARGON/TERMS OF ART

Every profession has its share of **jargon**, that specialized vocabulary used within a group with common backgrounds or interests. Naturally, the use of jargon can save time when it is understood by everyone within that group. Unfortunately, it can baffle those outside that intended group and not only waste readers' time but also create confusion and, ultimately, irritation.

Terms of art, on the other hand, are a shorthand to underlying concepts. Attorneys depend on terms of art for daily communication among themselves: *dictum, garnishment, fee simple.* Law students learn these terms for the legal concepts they are studying. But readers untrained in the law cannot be expected to understand these terms, and, interestingly, many specialized words within one area of law confuse even other lawyers. For instance, home insurance policies can bewilder antitrust lawyers.

Legal writers inadvertently use these specialized words and phrases in documents for laymen because they forget that others aren't familiar with the terms and their underlying concepts. Jargon, then, is a matter of **audience**. You need to meet your specific audience's needs with each choice of word, just as you meet their needs with your choices for organization and sentence structure. Your ultimate goal is to craft an understandable discussion for your anticipated audience: your professor on an exam; the judge or your classmates; your client who has a legal background; and your client who does not have a legal background.

SOLUTIONS

1. Identify and weed out **archaic legalisms**, i.e., words with plain English equivalents:

Archaic legalism	Plain English
aforesaid	previous
forthwith	immediately
henceforth	from now on
herein	in this document
hereinafter	after this
thereafter	after that, accordingly
therein	in
theretofore	up to that time
hitherto	before
viz.	that is, *or* for example
whereby	through, in accordance
said	the, that

2. Evaluate **coupled synonyms**, which were useful hundreds of years ago when three languages (French, Latin, and versions of Old English) were used simultaneously on one English island. Replace them, when practical, with one term your reader will understand.[2] For instance, instead of repeating "each and every," use only "each":

Coupled Synonyms

✗	acknowledge and confess	✗	act and deed
✗	aid and abet	✗	annul and set aside
✗	authorize and empower	✗	absolutely and completely
✗	deem and consider	✗	free and unfettered

---

[2] Be careful not to throw out necessary legal terms! For instance, "ready, willing, and able" are not legally redundant. Someone could be *willing* to share a document but not *ready* because the document has not been located. *See* Terri LeClercq, *Jargon: Manure, Margarine, and Moderation*, EXPERT LEGAL WRITING 119, 122 (1995).

51

✗	covenant and agree	✗	each and every
✗	due and payable	✗	each and all
✗	excess and unnecessary	✗	false and untrue
✗	final and conclusive	✗	full and complete
✗	fit and proper	✗	have and hold
✗	for and in consideration of	✗	force and effect
✗	fraud and deceit	✗	in truth and in fact
✗	void and of no effect	✗	let or hindrance
✗	for and during	✗	for and in consideration of
✗	give, devise, and bequeath	✗	keep and maintain
✗	last will and testament	✗	truth and veracity
✗	lot, tract, or parcel of land	✗	modified or changed
✗	null, void, and of no effect	✗	order and direct
✗	ordered, judged, and decreed	✗	save and except
✗	type and kind		

3. **Eliminate** unnecessary, **overused legal phrases** for parties' names and **replace** them with concrete references to case names, the parties' names, and specific pronouns.

Overused	**Suggested Replacements**
in this instant case	in this case, here (or use parties' names)
one must prove	the defendant must prove (or use name)
the court below	the trial [district] court
the said party	that party, the plaintiff [defendant]

WORDINESS

Legal documents frequently read as if the office copier has accidentally duplicated previous paragraphs. Because repetition results in lengthy documents and uninteresting reading, focus on your drafts with a hungry eye. Think back to "strong nouns and verbs." Then imagine how much more forceful your prose will be if you **cut a fourth** from your draft.

SOLUTIONS

1. Omit unnecessary **prepositions**.

> **X** Fred Fender read **through** the ACLU complaint **with regard to** his biggest client's employee-salary procedures. (16 words)

Fred Fender read ACLU's complaint **about** his biggest client's employee-salary procedures. (12 words)

> **X** **A provision of the** employee contracts required commission-only compensation. (10 words)

The **employee contracts' provision** required commission-only compensation. (8 words)

2. Replace unnecessary or ambiguous **passive voice** verbs. (*See also* Chapter 3, pp. 29–31.)

> **X** The contracts **had been signed** by each employee. (8 words)

Each **employee had signed** a contract. (6 words)

> **X** A contract cannot be voided, concluded Fender, simply because the salary result didn't meet the employee's expectations. (17 words, ambiguous)

Employees cannot void their own contracts simply because the salary didn't meet their expectations. (14 words, explicit)

3. Omit unnecessary **relative pronouns**.[3]

> **✗** Fender was the lawyer **who** drafted the original contract. (9 words)

Fender drafted the original contract. (5 words)

> **✗** He thought **that** he had plugged every possible hole **that** the employees might find. (14 words)

He thought he had plugged every hole the employees might find. (11 words)

4. Omit **throat-clearers**.

✗	obviously	✗	clearly
✗	manifestly	✗	to tell the truth
✗	as a matter of fact	✗	it is clear
✗	it is obvious that	✗	situation is where
✗	case is when		
✗	it would appear to be the case that		

> **✗** **It would appear to be the case** that he hadn't, but, **to tell the truth**, he didn't have the time now to waste responding to the ACLU's complaint. (28 words)

He hadn't, but he didn't have the time now to waste responding to the ACLU's complaint. (16 words)

---

[3] There is no iron-clad rule about the inclusion of "that," so common sense will have to tell you when you have used too many, or when, because you've omitted the "that," you have lost the coherence that a relative pronoun provided.

Fender thought **it was obvious that** the ACLU's complaint **was a waste of** everyone's time. (15 words)

Fender thought the ACLU's complaint wasted everyone's time. (8 words)

5. Replace **unnecessary expletives**, e.g., "there is," "there are," and "it is." Of course, some sentences need to begin with "there is": "There is no reason to worry about that indictment today." It is clumsy and even wordier to apply a hard-and-fast editing rule and thus create a monster: "No reason exists to worry about that indictment today." Ugh.

 There is no reason a famous lawyer should have to spend time on this nonsense. (15 words)

Famous lawyers need not spend time on this nonsense. (9 words)

 It was simple to add a "not" or a "no" to the original complaint and facts without researching further. (19 words, ambiguous subject)

Fender simply added a "not" or a "no" to the original complaint and facts without researching further. (17 words, strong subject/verb)

6. Avoid **unnecessary modification** unless it serves a tactical purpose.

 Creatively, he added **a very unique** introduction to **each and every** case the ACLU had cited. (16 words)

Creatively, he added a unique introduction to each case the ACLU had cited. (13 words, perhaps delete "creatively" as redundant)

7. Watch for **redundancy**. Modifying strong nouns might actually weaken them.

Redundant	Possible Revision
✗ alleged suspect	suspect
✗ consensus of opinion	consensus
✗ free gift	gift
✗ rather (or most) unique	unique
✗ the said party	that party, the defendants
✗ whether or not[4]	
✗ next subsequent	subsequent
✗ personal (or honest) opinion	opinion
✗ single most	most
✗ reason is because	reason is (*or* because)

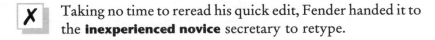 Taking no time to reread his quick edit, Fender handed it to the **inexperienced novice** secretary to retype.

Taking no time to reread his quick edit, Fender handed it to the **novice** secretary to retype.

NOUN STRINGS

Noun strings make legal writing dense and difficult. In a noun string, a succession of nouns modify each other; thus each preceding noun functions as an adjective that modifies the last noun:

Fender relied on brand new secretaries.
modifier modifier noun

Until readers locate the noun (secretaries), they must assume that each word they come across in the noun slot **functions** as a noun. After

---

[4] "Whether or not" is usually redundant: *We do not know **whether or not** the executive summary will bring you immediate benefits (unnecessary "or not"*). But like most "rules," this one does not cover all possibilities: *Agency fees are collected to defray expenses of the activities of the union, expenses that benefit all members of the collective bargaining unit, **whether union members or not**.* Here the "or not" is syntactically necessary to complete the thought.

reading "brand" and "new," readers are confused. They waste time and patience reprocessing all the modifiers into adjectives that describe "secretaries." If one modifier is already an adverb, then the hyphen is unnecessary.

Here is an example of an unwitting but incorrect noun string that cost a supply clerk his job: a site contractor called, asking the clerk to send a number of support bars to a construction site. Over the phone, the contractor asked, "Tomorrow morning, will you deliver ten, foot-long concrete bars?" The clerk agreed and wrote on the order "ten foot long concrete bars" plus the address, etc. The next morning, the loading team arrived with bars — bars that the contractor refused. Why? Look at the difference between these terms, and imagine the confused result:

- ten foot-long concrete bars
- ten-foot-long concrete bars

The error cost both time and supplies — and thus the clerk's job.

SOLUTIONS

1. Insert a **hyphen** to connect two or more adjectives before a noun.
big-business law firms
one-time tax refund

2. Unstring the noun string.

✗	a gross receipt sales tax	• a gross-receipt sales tax
		• a sales tax on gross receipts
✗	new financial institutions franchises	• new financial-institutions franchises
		• franchises for new financial institutions

NOMINALIZATIONS/CONCRETE WORDS

Many a strong verb or concrete noun is hidden beneath a **nominalization,** those multisyllabic words with Latinate suffixes and prefixes:

✗	ize	✗	osity
✗	ate	✗	ability
✗	tion	✗	ancy
✗	ion	✗	al
✗	ence	✗	ive
✗	ment	✗	mis-

Some examples are investiga**tion,** necess**itate,** intellig**ence, mis**appropriate.

Although grammatically correct, nominalizations dilute a sentence by implying, rather than stating, the logical who/what relationships in the sentence.

✗ One of the ACLU lawyers made an **investigation** of the original filing.

An ACLU lawyer **investigated** the original filing.

✗ Despite the clerk's **protestations,** the ACLU lawyer's insistence took the highlighted pages before the judge.

Although the clerk **protested,** the ACLU lawyer **insisted** the judge review the highlighted pages, and he did.

SOLUTIONS

1. Watch for and replace nouns created **from stronger verbs:**

Nominalization	Verb Form
determination	to determine

resolution	to resolve
utilization	to use
reinforcement	to enforce
the addition of	to add
assumption	to assume
continuation	to continue

2. Also watch for and replace nouns created from **adjectives** (that were themselves once stronger verbs):

Noun/Adjective	Original Verb
enforceability/enforceable	enforce
applicability/applicable	apply
specificity/specific	specify

TREACHEROUS WORDS

Choosing the exact and necessary word is hard, deliberate work. Some words elude us as we draft; others sound correct in a context but aren't; some words are incorrect in any context. No one knows the meaning of every word or when to use each word he or she does know. But in legal writing, it is essential to review the shades of difference between synonyms, for instance, and to keep track of those words you frequently misuse.

Textual ambiguity

X Promulgating rules to maintain integrity is a key element in the legal profession **which** distinguishes it from some other professions.

Interpretation 1.   The writer intended to emphasize only the promulgating as a key element of <u>the profession</u>, so she needed a comma after "profession."

Interpretation 2. The writer intended to point out that <u>promulgating rules</u> distinguishes it from other professions and thus should have replaced the "which" with "that" to signal an essential and necessary clause. See Chapter 5, p. 76, and the following mini-dictionary.

Misused words:

1. **affect/effect:** *Affect* is a verb, meaning to influence or to assume the appearance of. *Effect* is a noun, meaning the result. (*Effect* can also be a verb meaning "to make a change" or "to accomplish.")
2. **alternative/option, choice:** If you have two choices, *each* is an alternative to the other. Traditionally, linguists have held that with more than two options, you have *options* or *choices* but not an *alternative*. (Contemporary linguists no longer hold tightly to this distinction.)
3. **among/between:** *Among* refers to groups of three and more; *between* functions as a distinction between only two.

   Among the many functions of a lawyer is taking yearly CLE courses. *Between* client pressure and billing-hours pressure, some lawyers are tempted to cut ethical corners.

   Between and *among* require objective pronouns:

   Between you and *me*, I can't stand to witness fights between *him* and *her*. Among *us*, the custom is to bring cookies to the office once a week.

4. **as/because:** *As* is a comparative, like *like*. *Because* signals causality.

    Incorrect: *As* he didn't attend many classes, his classmates thought he had dropped the course.

   Correct: *Because* he didn't attend many classes, his classmates thought he had dropped the course.

Correct: The Defendant can be *as* sincere *as* a nun, but *because* she has her dates wrong, she will not be believed.

5. **assume/presume**: To *assume* is to take for granted that something is true or accurate. To *presume* is to take upon oneself without leave or warrant, to dare or go beyond what is right or proper. Note the use of the root in *presumption*.

6. **assure/insure/ensure**: All three of these words mean to make certain or safe, so their precise use is complicated. You *assure* people (removing doubt and suspense). You *insure* with money and guarantees (and insurance policies). And you *ensure* when you are making things certain or safe, e.g., *ensure* your child's safety with a seat belt.

7. **because/since**: Traditionally, these words signaled different meanings and were not interchangeable. Although it is not technically incorrect to use them interchangeably now, it will benefit a legal writer to limit *since* to signal time, and *because* to signal causality.

8. **bimonthly/semimonthly**: Most writers resort to using "every two months" or "twice a month." For the record, though, *bi* means two; *semi* means half. Thus, *bimonthly* is every two months, and *semimonthly* is twice a month.

9. **continuous/continual**: *Continual* means frequently occurring; *continuous* means occurring without interference.

   The lawyer had to sit through a two-hour, *continuous* CLE class on ethics. A disgruntled participant on the back row offered *continual* interruptions.

10. **composed/comprised**: *Composed* means made of (the parts compose the whole), and *comprised* means contains (the whole comprises the parts).

    The audience is *composed of* people with varied backgrounds. The symphony hall *comprises* people with varied backgrounds.

11. **currently/presently**: Although the nouns *current* and *present* are basically synonymous, the adverb forms traditionally signal a difference in time.

We are *currently* (right now) studying word choice. *Presently* (in the very near future) we will stop and take a break.

12. **different than/different from**: Things *differ from* each other. *Different than* is considered incorrect unless using "from" creates bulky, illogical phraseology following it.

Fender's brief was not *different from* the ACLU's.

I agree that the Supreme Court has interpreted the United States Constitution very *differently than* the Founders intended and that courts err on the side of tyranny.

13. **discreet/discrete**: A *discreet* investigator is tactful and judicious, careful. In contrast, an investigator may be *discrete* from other witnesses at the trial, meaning that he is disconnected from them, separate and distinct.

14. **disinterested/uninterested**: A judge or stenographer is *disinterested* in a case; that is, the judge has no personal involvement in it and yet needs to know the details of the case. The court clerk may truly be *uninterested*, that is, not engaged by the elements of the story:

The law student was totally uninterested in the guest lecturer, so she fell asleep.

15. **hopefully**: Traditionally, *hopefully* functioned as an adverb meaning "with hope." Thus, "Hopefully it will rain" ambiguously suggested that the speaker is hoping for rain or, technically, that it will rain hope. Following today's modern general-usage rule, dictionaries now allow this ambiguity. Thus you will discover that currently "hopefully" can also mean "I or we hope." Because the option produces an ambiguity, careful writers stick to the traditional rule and limit its use.

16. **i.e./e.g.**: *I.e.* (*id est*) means "that is" and indicates that an inclusive list or statement will follow. *E.g.* (*exempli gratia*) means "for example" and signals that the author is including an example or

examples with the introductory statement. Each is followed by a comma.

Lawyers must accept responsibility; i.e., they must find clients, perform some research and writing, and keep track of billable hours.
Lawyers must accept some responsibility; e.g., they must find clients.

17. imply/infer: To *imply* is to hint at something. To *infer* is to suggest an intimate or incriminating connection.

He *implied* that she was not telling the truth when he asked to see her list of references.
He *inferred* that his client was angry because she never looked directly at him across the table.

18. it's/its: *It's* easy to distinguish these two forms if you can remember that the apostrophe signals that a letter is left out, so the form *it's* has to be an abbreviation for *it is*. Following that rule will force its competitor, *its*, into its only logical slot, as a third-person singular pronoun like *his* or *her*.

19. lay/lie: *Lay* means to place or put and usually takes an object (transitive verb). Past tense: laid. Perfect: laid. *Lie* means recline (intransitive verb). Past tense: lay. Perfect: lain.

She *laid* her casebooks on the table.
He *lay* awake all night before the exam.

20. prescribe/proscribe: You *prescribe* when you are giving a remedy or a decree. The opposite is true of *proscribe*, when you are forbidding, prohibiting.

21. reluctant/reticent: If a law student is *reluctant* to join a study group, he is unwilling or will grudgingly consent. That he is *reticent*, however, means he does not reveal his feelings readily.

22. that/which: When you draft an essential (restrictive) clause that will not be "punctuated out" of the sentence with commas, use *that.* When you want the information to be merely descriptive, nonessential to the sentence's meaning, use two commas and *which.*

The clause *that* explained the rule is not punctuated.
The clause, *which* merely offered the background of the rule, disappeared from the main text because it was set off with commas.

23. **who/which:** If your antecedent is inanimate (nonhuman), use *that* or *which* as a pronoun. If the antecedent is a person, use *who.* The question becomes more complicated when you are referring, for instance, to an agency filled with people. If you are referring to the agency as a whole, use *which*; if the people within the agency are the center of your sentence or its intent, use *who* and *whom.*

24. **who/whom:** Student writers aren't comfortable with whom, because they are uncomfortable with the distinction between subject and object forms of pronouns — and thus they edit any sentence out that may create an error. Use objective pronouns when the word is the direct or indirect object, or object of a preposition: I told him (direct object) to stop. I gave *him* (indirect object) the assignment. We gave the assignment to *him* (object of preposition). The trick is to substitute he/him (or she/her) for the missing word who/whom, and you will choose the correct form. Thus: Police are looking for a man who/whom was involved in an afternoon collision. Ask yourself: he/him was involved in, and you'll substitute correctly. Police are looking for a man *who* was involved in an afternoon collision.

SOLUTIONS

1. Consult **professional sources** like Wilson Follett, *Modern American Usage: A Guide*; W.H. Fowler, *A Dictionary of Modern English Usage*; David Mellinkoff, *Mellinkoff's Dictionary of American Legal Usage*. Using them, **study** those words frequently misused.

2. Create **your own list** of words that confuse you or that you frequently misuse. Keep the list in your computer's thesaurus or print out a list and keep it near your writing area.

What to Remember

- Remember your audience: edit for **legal jargon** that is not appropriate.
- Delete redundant, **unnecessary words**.
- Edit from the concluding sentence to the first, examining **pronouns** for their proper antecedents.
- Properly hyphenate **strings of nouns and adjectives** or break up the string.
- Edit to replace **nominalizations**.
- Review our list of frequently **misused words**.

CONCLUDING EXERICISES: WORDS

See answers, pp. 107–109.

ALSO REVIEW EXERCISES ON ACCOMPANYING CD.

Which of these phrases and sentences can be shortened and yet not substantially changed?

1. for the purpose of evaluating

2. The judge went on to say that he had never seen such a blatant use of another's work.

3. The obligation of Fender existed in a legal way, and probably also in a moral way.

Find common terminology and shorter phrases to replace the following jargon.

4. Fred Fender absolutely refuted this charge. The said party contended also that he has been unfairly persecuted and enjoined into a morass that his secretary was responsible for.

5. Fender pointed to various defenses, to wit: the pressure of time, his inexperienced secretarial pool, the length of the ACLU filing.

Separate nouns and add connecting words or hyphens as necessary.

6. postage guaranteed envelopes

7. deeply frightened secretary

8. clerk's new heightened awareness

9. well established code of conduct

10. big firm CLE compliance

Identify any nominalizations, and rewrite to clarify the who/did what/to whom action that has been implied.

11. A thorough investigation of the two, similar filings necessitated that the clerk work late.

12. The next morning a presentation was made to the judge that was full reinforcement of the ACLU's research.

13. His new public resolution to do his own work was merely the continuation of a lifetime of living on the edge.

Correct the examples in this concluding quiz that mixes the word problems you've just reviewed. Look for jargon, wordiness, pronoun antecedents, noun strings, nominalizations, and treacherous words.

14. It was very unique for an attorney to address the court and the public about his error.

15. Fender thanked the court for allowing him to make a public presentation of his new-found, original writing skills in a CLE class.

16. When the judge found the clerk in the office at 7:30 a.m., he worried that he was there too early.

17. This type and kind of dishonesty reflected on the truth and veracity of any big-time lawyer and on the court.

18. The obligation of the attorney may have existed whether or not the document was an official court filing.

19. The overly-confident law firm had no document review system to catch this problem.

20. It is important to note that the signature at the bottom of a legal document is an acceptance by the attorney of professional responsibility for the writing, and the secretary cannot be held responsible for its content, which is consistent with our understanding of all professional documents.

21. When an attorney only works for himself, he has no one else to blame for errors.

22. After researching for any other similar cases, there appear to be several instances of plagiarism in other jurisdictions that the judge discovered and dealt with publicly.

23. The judge found for the ACLU and ordered a strict scrutiny of all of Fender's firm's documents. This was followed by a public announcement.

24. Let us just say that this firm will also penalize Mr. Fender and will not allow this sloppy writing to be duplicated in the future.

Circle the correct word.

25. The firm considered him to be a rainmaker as/because he had brought in three major clients in three years.

26. The new secretary had never been asked to be discrete/discreet about the document makeover.

27. This new secretary did not know its/it's consequences, but soon learned.

28. The managing partner, however, had to assure/insure/ensure that the firm was safe from any criticism from the legal community.

29. Any seasoned secretary would have been able to imply/infer from the markings on the draft that there was something wrong.

30. The firm had continuous/continual CLE classes on ethics.

Investigate the word choice in these examples. Eliminate repetitions and edit for ambiguous or misused words.

31. In the instant case before him, the judge knew he had to make a decision with regard to his own understanding of ethics.

32. It is not normal for a judge to begin a day with a sanction.

33. The judge considered a number of punishments, i.e., CLE classes, a two-month bar from his court, a close scrutiny of every document that firm filed, etc.

A world that has only periods is a world without inflections. It is world without shade. It has a music without sharps and flats. It is a martial music. It has a jackboot rhythm. Words cannot bend and curve. A comma, by comparison, catches the gentle drift of the mind in thought, turning in on itself and back on itself, reversing, redoubling and returning along the course of its own sweet river music; while the semicolon brings clauses and thoughts together with all the silent discretion of a hostess arranging guests around her dinner table.
- *Pico Iyer, That Humble Comma, Time, June 13, 1988*

✦ ✦ ✦ ✦

5

PUNCTUATING WITH STYLE

This is your last look at your draft: return to that organized, polished document you're creating, and this time review the punctuation. Punctuation marks hold together, separate, and set the pace and meaning of your document. When early writers added punctuation to their speeches in the third century B.C., they did so to signal places for them to pause when they read aloud. The different marks they developed signaled the reader/speaker's pause length; obviously, there aren't many options for pacing speech. That is part of the reason why today's punctuation is governed by only a few rules.

Punctuation reflects style when you deliberately choose punctuation marks to reflect your intent. Your intention might be to pushwordstogether or to string them far apart. But of course you can't write like that. So that's where style comes in — your deliberate choice of marks will make readers speed up, or slow down, at appropriate places.

First review and memorize the actual rules below, which have been broken into two sets of rules:

- General punctuation rules
- Specific legal-writing punctuation rules

Then experiment with punctuation options, creating and developing your own style so that readers can easily depend on your punctuation.

GENERAL PUNCTUATION RULES

1. Complete sentence.

The basic purpose of the Fourth Amendment is to safeguard the privacy and security of individuals against arbitrary invasion by government officials.

2. Complete sentence; complete sentence.

The basic purpose of the Fourth Amendment is to safeguard the privacy and security of individuals against arbitrary invasion by government officials; a search conducted without a warrant based on probable cause is "per se unreasonable" and subject only to "specific and well-defined exceptions." *Katz v. United States*, 389 U.S. 347, 357 (1967).

3. Complete sentence; *conjunctive adverb,* complete sentence.

; therefore,
; however,
; nevertheless,
; consequently,
; furthermore,

The basic purpose of the Fourth Amendment is to safeguard the privacy and security of individuals against arbitrary invasion by government officials; **indeed,** a search conducted without a warrant based on probable cause is "per se unreasonable" and subject only to "specific and well-defined exceptions." *Katz v. United States*, 389 U.S. 347, 357 (1967).

4. Complete   *, interruptor,*   sentence.

, on the other hand,
, for example,
, in fact,

If a search is, **in fact,** conducted pursuant to voluntary consent, then that consent is a legal exception.

5. *Adverb*   incomplete sentence, complete sentence.

Although
After
Because
While
When

When a search is conducted without a probable-cause warrant, that search is "per se unreasonable."

6. *Short introductory phrase,* complete sentence. (optional but useful comma)

With few exceptions the search may be deemed "reasonable."

With few exceptions, the search may be deemed "reasonable."

7. Complete sentence   *adverb*   incomplete sentence. (no comma)

although
after
because
while
when

A search is "per se unreasonable" **when** a search is conducted without a probable-cause warrant.

8. *Dates* containing both day and year require *two commas*.

The car's driver will appear in court July 15, 2007, to argue the passenger's consent to search the car.

The car's driver will appear in court July 2007 to argue the passenger's consent to search the car. (contains only a month)

9. *Hyphens* combine two adjectives before a noun, or a string of nouns before the main noun: (*See* Chapter 4, p. 57)

A guilt-ridden passenger had revealed the hidden knife under the car seat.

Remember, however, that adverbs ending in -ly should never be hyphenated.

10. *Dashes* signal a break in thought and writing.

The driver had refused the search—not even remembering the knife under her seat.

Dashes differ from hyphens in both typography and purpose. Dashes are typed with two hyphens and no spaces on either side. Dashes *separate*; hyphens *draw together*.

11. *Apostrophes* signal possessives, not plurals.

The police officers' consent was aimed at both women. (more than one officer)

The driver's refusal came when the officers said they would impound the car. (one driver)

English pronouns have their own possessive case (his, my, their, our) and **do not** require an apostrophe.

 The United States Supreme Court gave **it's** limitations for the Miranda warnings.

Nouns, even numbers and letters, do not use apostrophes to create plurals.

 The occupant's had been speeding in a residential area.

All winners of the 100s were given a one-hundred-dollar bill.

In the 1970s a series of cases rejected requiring police to advise individuals of the right to refuse consent.

12. *Colons* follow a complete sentence that concludes with a dramatic saying, a separated list, or a list that completes a sentence:

Dramatic saying: Ghandi admitted to authorities that he knew a lot about prisons: African and Indian.

Separated list: If writers choose to create a list that follows a complete sentence but is **not** a part of the textual sentence's grammar, then they should follow the following seven conventions:

1. Colon introduction.
2. Indentation.
3. Grammatical parallel.
4. Capital letters.
5. Numbered items.
6. Periods at the end of each item.
7. No "or" or "and" for culmination.

List completing sentence: When a list is a grammatical part of the sentence, the items to be enumerated must belong to the same class, with a common idea introduced before the colon. Then, if writers want, they can keep the items within the text: (1) by introducing the list with a colon; (2) by indenting all of each item and numbering each item; (3) by beginning each item with a lowercase letter; (4) by concluding each item but the last with a semicolon; (5) by placing a semicolon and "and" or "or" after the next-to-last item; and (6) by concluding the final item with a period unless the list does not conclude the textual sentence.

Or writers can choose to separate that same list with white space and an indented list:

1. by introducing the list with a colon;
2. by indenting all of each item and numbering each item;
3. by beginning each item with a lowercase letter;
4. by concluding each item but the last with a semicolon;
5. by placing a semicolon and "and" or "or" after the next-to-last item; and
6. by concluding the final item with a period unless the list does not conclude the textual sentence.

Do not use a colon after a verb or a preposition.

 A suspect has: no right to a Miranda concerning searches. (delete colon)

 The police were nevertheless criticized for: arresting two soccer moms, threatening to keep them beyond their children's school hours, and taking them to the jail because they found a cake knife. (delete colon)

Capitalization after a colon is optional, but most writers capitalize *complete* sentences after the colon and leave fragments in lowercase:

This has been a lesson for all neighborhood mothers: keep your cake knives in view.

13. *Quotation marks* around commas and periods, like "these," must go outside a comma or period.

The car's driver insisted, "We have been to a birthday party."

14. *Quotation marks* around colons and semicolons go "inside"; this rule is an American rule.

The passenger reported that she had been terrified of the "flashing blue and red lights"; she is now under sedation.

15. *Items in a series require* commas between items *and* before the "and" or "or" in technical writing.

The women had assumed people could get arrested only for breaking and entering, assault and battery, and rape.

16. *Semicolons* are necessary for a list that contains a *comma within a list* of items. In these lists, you might think of the semicolons as a monster comma.

The United States Supreme Court specifically rejected requiring police officers to advise of the right to refuse consent; dismissed as difficult, if not impractical, a new, detailed warning; and concluded that the searches are a normal occurrence on streets, in offices, and in homes.

SPECIFIC LEGAL-WRITING RULES

17. Sentence, *conjunction* sentence.

, *and*
, *or*
, *nor*
, *but*
, *yet*

75

This comma with a simple conjunction is not essential, but legal writers depend on it to signal a new subject/verb.

18. Complete, citation, sentence.

In the seminal case, <u>Schneckloth v. Bustamonte</u>, 412 U.S. 218, 231 (1973), the United States Supreme Court divided Miranda warnings from consent to search.

Similar to Rule 4 above, the citation is an interruptor and requires a comma before and after it to signal readers that the interruption is over and the main textual line will continue.

19. *That and which clauses* are punctuated, or not, as essential clauses (that) and essential clauses (which). (*See* Chapter 4, p. 63–64.)

a. Federal authority <u>that requires informing</u> a suspect of his rights is covered under Miranda.
   b. Some federal authority, <u>which requires informing a suspect of his rights</u>, is covered under Miranda.

In example a, the <u>clause</u> is essential to narrowing or limiting which authority is covered. In example b, the <u>clause</u> helps describe which of "some" authority is covered but isn't essential to let readers know which of "some" is covered.
   Notice that the essential clause does not have commas punctuating it "out" of the main text. The clause is needed there to establish meaning. Notice, too, that the nonessential clause must be punctuated out of the main text with two commas. So, if the clause begins with "which," it should be nonessential and punctuated out.

20. *Quotations* more than 49 words in length are indented and single-spaced.[1]

---

[1] ASSOCIATION OF LEGAL WRITING DIRECTORS & DARBY DICKERSON, ALWD CITATION MANUAL: A PROFESSIONAL SYSTEM OF CITATION R. 47.5(a) (3d ed., Aspen L. & Bus. 2006); THE BLUEBOOK: A UNIFORM SYSTEM OF CITATION R. 5.1 (18th ed., 2005).

According to legal editors,

> If the quotation is longer than 49 words (or if you have a special reason for setting quoted material outside your main text), signal the indented quotation with a single-spaced indented format but do *not* use quotation marks: the formatting signals the direct quotation. If the quotation is not a part of your textual sentence, lead into it with a colon. If the quotation picks up your textual syntax, do not add any punctuation before indenting and single spacing.

[Footnote would be required here.]

21. *Ellipses and spacing* indicate that you have omitted material from a passage being quoted. (A legal ellipsis mark is composed of *three spaced* periods.)[2]

A 1973 Supreme Court case set the standard:

> One alternative . . . would be to advise him of that right before eliciting his consent. That . . . would be thoroughly impractical. . . . Consent searches are part of the standard investigatory techniques of law enforcement agencies. They normally occur on the highway, or in a person's home or office, and under informal and unstructured conditions.

Schneckloth v. Bustamonte, 412 U.S. 218, 231-32 (1973).

When you omit material after a period within the original text, add a fourth dot as the final punctuation. (See the last ellipsis above.) If you omit material before the sentence ends, follow it with white space before the first dot. (See the third ellipsis above.) You should have a complete sentence on both sides of a four-dot ellipsis. Most legal writers do not use ellipsis points before a block quotation beginning with a complete sentence even though they have (usually) left out material from the original.

---

[2] ALWD CITATION MANUAL R. 48.4; BLUEBOOK R. 5.2(a).

22. *Brackets* signal change in quoted material:

(a) missing words or letters;

(b) capitals changed to lowercase and lowercased words changed to capitals to fit your own sense of the quotation into your text;

(c) additions that help explain ambiguous material in a quotation;

(d) your own comments inserted into quoted material; and

(e) the word "sic" to indicate an error repeated from the original ("sic" is a complete word meaning "in this manner" or "thus").

Following are examples of correctly placed brackets:

The women's defense was that their "weapon was only a [kitchen] knife used to cut birthday cakes."

"[S]ubject of a search does have the right to refuse consent to a search," reminded the court.

What to Remember

- Choose punctuation marks that help the reader understand the substantive material, pulling words together and apart appropriately.
- Review the general punctuation list and make necessary adjustments.
- Double-check those marks required specifically for legal writers.
- Check Bluebook/ALWD manuals to ensure your marks conform to expected legal form and format.

CONCLUDING EXERCISES: **PUNCTUATION**

See answers, pp. 109–110.
ALSO REVIEW EXERCISES ON ACCOMPANYING **CD.**

Grade yourself on correcting these concluding quizzes that mix the punctuation rules you have just reviewed.

1. In Dallas a 16 year old kid with a decidedly-red convertible was stopped for speeding.

2. He pulled over to the side of the road. And was so nervous he hit the curb.

3. "Ohmygod no", the policeman heard him chanting.

4. "This will be an easy stop," the policeman said into his car speaker; "because he is already admitting he's in trouble."

5. First he walked completely around the car, noting its condition, stopped by the passenger window and asked to see the boy's driver's license.

6. He asked for information — the driver's name, owner of the vehicle, where the driver was going, and if he knew he was exceeding the speed limit.

7. The police officer said,
"You have the right to not answer these simple questions, but I advise you to."

8. When the boy quickly spouted the answers the police officer wrote several of them down, and grunted at the rest.

9. The process needed to go quickly which the officer knew from experience.

10. Some speeders will become indignant and argumentative and some will be embarrassed and just want to sign the forms and leave.

6
FORMATTING FOR A VISUAL SOCIETY

Remember the advice in the *Message to Students*: Your readers are not going to look at your document because they have extra time or because they need entertainment. Rather, they need information — and fast. To help them find that information, writers should make each document as attractive and accessible as possible. You are already the victim of the subliminal seduction of law schools: All opinions look like each other, and all sample memoranda look like other sample memoranda. You need to remember your own dismay at your first sight of these documents and break the pattern of your own pages by making them

- visually inviting,
- organized so that they can be read and understood quickly, and
- understandable on the first reading.

Solutions

1. Add **white space** throughout the document with margins, spaces between paragraphs, space around tabulation, graphics.
2. Create an **initial road map** that contains both the conclusion and brief road map of what will follow.
3. Adjust **paragraphs' lengths** so that they are not all the same (long) length.
4. Include **side bars** for summaries or headings for client documents.
5. Include **graphics** where possible, and label them so readers can skim the accompanying text.
6. Avoid **ALL CAPITAL LETTERS** where possible (don't change trademark names, or capital/strikeout system of some legislation).
7. Use an **appendix** for explanatory material.
8. Study **proximity, alignment, repetition, and contrast,** and apply these techniques where possible.[1]

---

[1] ROBIN WILLIAMS, THE NON-DESIGNER'S DESIGN BOOK (Peachtree Press, 1994). Thanks to Ruth Anne Robbins, Rutgers School of Law–Camden, for re-acquainting me with this valuable resource.

Example 1A. A student memorandum without visual cueing

QUESTION PRESENTED: Does an attorney commit malpractice when he cites a case that has been overturned and this results in an adverse decision in litigation?

CONCLUSION: Yes. An attorney who cites an overturned case does not act as a reasonably prudent attorney. If the failure results in harm to the client, the attorney is negligent and thus has committed malpractice.

FACTS: Our client, Lima, Inc., an importer of limes, was represented by John Gerardi in a litigation matter. In his brief, Gerardi relied heavily on a case that, unknown to him, the Texas Supreme Court had overturned six months before Lima's scheduled hearing.

. . . .

DISCUSSION: Lima's malpractice claim against Gerardi hinges on the legal issue of negligence, particularly the extent of Gerardi's duty to research the law properly and the breach of this duty. In Texas, a malpractice claim is based on the law of negligence. Cosgrove v. Grimes, 774 S.W.2d 662, 664 (Tex. 1989). To show that Gerardi was negligent, Lima must show that Gerardi had a duty to Lima, that he breached it, and that this breach was the proximate cause of Lima's harm. Cosgrove, 774 S.W.2d at 665. An attorney has a duty to properly research the law and breaches this duty when he fails to do so. Morrill v. Graham, 27 Tex. 646, 651 (1864); Walder v. Texas, 85 S.W.3d 824, 827 (Tex. App. — Waco 2002).

(margin note: good road map but not highlighted)

. . . .

An attorney has a duty to properly research the law and breaches this duty when he fails to do so. When a lawyer undertakes a matter on behalf of a client, the lawyer must exercise ordinary care and diligence in handling the client's matter, including using the skills normally possessed by competent lawyers. Savings Bank v. Ward, 100 U.S. 195, 199 (1879). The lawyer breaches his duty to his client when he fails to meet this standard. Savings Bank, 100 U.S. at 199.

(margin note: no headings)

. . . .

Checking cases to see whether they are still reliable precedent is a central part of a lawyer's responsibility. The Texas rules of professional responsibility require a lawyer to be able to undertake "the analysis of precedent" to be considered competent. Tex. Disciplinary Rules of Prof'l. Conduct, R. 1.01 cmt. 3 (2002).

(margin note: no visual cues)

. . . .

Gerardi may argue that because the case he relied on was only recently overturned, the law in that area is unsettled, so failure to account for it is not a breach. Where a particular area of law is unsettled, an attorney will not be held liable for failing to know it. Morrill, 27 Tex. at 652. In Morrill, an attorney failed to present a claim against a decedent's estate within the proper time period. The Texas Supreme Court ruled that the attorney was not negligent in failing to do so because the question of whether the presentment was required was an "open and controverted point." Morrill, 27 Tex. at 652.

. . . .

Where the attorney's breach of duty proximately causes harm to his client, the attorney will be liable for malpractice. Two Thirty Nine Joint Venture v. Joe, 60 S.W.3d 896, 909 (Tex. App. — Dallas 2001, pet. granted). To show causation, we must show that Lima would have won the case but for Gerardi's breach of duty and that this was foreseeable, i.e., that Gerardi should have anticipated that his failure to research properly would cause injury to his client. Two Thirty Nine Joint Venture, 60 S.W.3d at 909.

. . . .

Because Geraldi had a duty and breached it, and because that breach was the proximate cause of injury, all of the elements of negligence are present. Thus, Lima may sustain a malpractice action against Gerardi.

Example 1B. Student memorandum with headings, white space, and initial road map

QUESTION PRESENTED: Does an attorney commit malpractice when he cites a case that has been overturned and this results in an adverse decision in litigation?

CONCLUSION: Yes. An attorney who cites an overturned case does not act as a reasonably prudent attorney. If the failure results in harm to the client, the attorney is negligent and thus has committed malpractice.

FACTS: Our client, Lima, Inc., an importer of limes, was represented by John Gerardi in a litigation matter. In his brief, Gerardi relied heavily on a case that, unknown to him, the Texas Supreme Court had overturned six months before Lima's scheduled hearing. Lima lost the case and was forced to pay $250,000 in damages. The court explicitly made its decision based on Gerardi's reliance on the overturned decision and admonished Gerardi for his failure to Shepardize. Lima has engaged us to sue Gerardi for malpractice.

DISCUSSION: Lima's malpractice claim against Gerardi hinges on the legal issue of negligence, particularly the extent of Gerardi's duty to research the law properly and the breach of this duty. In Texas, a malpractice claim is based on the law of negligence. Cosgrove v. Grimes, 774 S.W.2d 662, 664 (Tex. 1989). To show that Gerardi was negligent, Lima must show

    (1) that Gerardi had a duty to Lima, that he breached it, and
    (2) that this breach was the proximate cause of Lima's harm. Cosgrove, 774 S.W.2d at 665.

    An attorney has a duty to properly research the law and breaches this duty when he fails to do so. Morrill v. Graham, 27 Tex. 646, 651 (1864);

alignment — all major headings are flush left

conclusion up front

legal issue (negligence) as first sentence, followed by setup with indented, **aligned** numbers and boldfaced numbers

84

<u>Walder v. Texas</u>, 85 S.W.3d 824, 827 (Tex. App. — Waco 2002). Failure to check legal precedents is a breach of this duty. <u>Two Thirty Nine Joint Venture v. Joe</u>, 60 S.W.3d 896, 905 (Tex. App. — Dallas 2001, pet. granted); Tex. Disciplinary Rules of Prof'l Conduct R. 1.01 cmt. 3 (2002). Where the breach proximately causes harm to the client, the attorney will be liable for malpractice. <u>Two Thirty Nine Joint Venture</u>, 60 S.W.3d at 896.

1. Duty and Breach

An attorney has a duty to properly research the law and breaches this duty when he fails to do so. When a lawyer undertakes a matter on behalf of a client, the lawyer must exercise ordinary care and diligence in handling the client's matter, including using the skills normally possessed by competent lawyers. <u>Savings Bank v. Ward</u>, 100 U.S. 195, 199 (1879). The lawyer breaches his duty to his client when . . .

. . . .

Counteranalysis

Gerardi may argue that because the case he relied on was only recently overturned, the law in that area is unsettled, so failure to account for it is not a breach. Where a particular area of law is unsettled, an attorney will not be held liable for failing to know it. <u>Morrill</u>, 27 Tex. at 652. In <u>Morrill</u>, an attorney failed to present a claim against a decedent's estate within the proper time period. The Texas Supreme Court ruled that the attorney was not negligent in failing to do so because the question of whether the presentment was required was an "open and controverted point." <u>Morrill</u>, 27 Tex. at 652.

. . . .

2. Breach Is Proximate Cause

Where the attorney's breach of duty proximately causes harm to his client, the attorney will be liable for malpractice. <u>Two Thirty Nine Joint Venture</u>, 60 S.W.3d at 909. To show causation, we must show that Lima would have won the case but for Gerardi's breach of duty and that this was foreseeable, i.e., that Gerardi should have anticipated that his failure to research properly would cause injury to his client. <u>Two Thirty Nine Joint Venture</u>, 60 S.W.3d at 909. Normally, . . .

. . . .

Conclusion

Because Geraldi had a duty and breached it, and because that breach was the proximate cause of injury, all of the elements of negligence are present. Thus, Lima may sustain a malpractice action against Gerardi.

Margin notes:

headings follow setup

repetition of indented left major headings, **contrasting** boldface

analysis shifts to other perspective

second prong of setup; **repetition** of numbers

repetition of setup and legal question

Example 2A. Client letter emphasizing content only

August 22, 2007

VIA FEDERAL EXPRESS
Dean Katherine S. Broderick
David A. Clark School of Law
University of the District of Columbia
4200 Connecticut Avenue, N.W.
Building 38, Room 201
Washington, D.C. 20008

Dear Dean Broderick:

no identifying
information

dense information
block with no
hierarchy

Please find enclosed a Subpoena Duces Tecum Without Deposition
which has been issued by the U.S. District Court, Middle District of
Florida, Jacksonville Division, Case No. 99-978-Civ-J-11D, for any and all
documents regarding Lillian Lander (DOB: 9/16/46; SSN: 458-48-3195).
We would appreciate your providing any and all items in the attached
subpoena. These documents should include a complete statement of all
opinions expressed and the basis and reasons therefor; the data or other
information considered in forming the opinion(s); any exhibits to be used as
a summary of or support for the opinion(s); expert qualifications, including
a list of all publications authored within the preceding ten years (include
your resume); compensation amount(s); and a list of cases in which you
have testified as an expert at trial or by deposition within the preceding
four years.

reader skimming
quickly would
assume all writer
needs is invoice

Please submit your statement for reproduction charges, and we will
reimburse you that same amount. Thank you for your assistance in this
matter. Please do not hesitate to call if you require further information.

Yours truly,

Annabel Garcia
Legal Assistant

Example 2B. Revised client letter: white space, tabulation, contrast

---

August 22, 2007

VIA FEDERAL EXPRESS
Dean Katherine S. Broderick
David A. Clark School of Law
University of the District of Columbia
4200 Connecticut Avenue, N.W.
Building 38, Room 201
Washington, D.C. 20008

RE: Lillian Lander v. Al Kayda
Case No. 99-978-Civ-J-11D

> bold **contrast**
> provides context

Dear Dean Broderick:

We are asking that you comply with the Subpoena Duces Tecum Without Deposition in this case. The U.S. District Court, Middle District of Florida, Jacksonville Division, asks for any and all documents regarding Lillian Lander (DOB: 9/16/46; SSN: 458-48-3195). Please provide any items in the attached subpoena, including:

> active, up-front request

1. **opinions** expressed and the basis of their reasoning;
2. **data or other information** considered in forming the opinion(s);
3. **exhibits** to be used as a summary of or support for the opinion(s);
4. **expert qualifications,** including a list of all publications authored within the preceding ten years (include your resume);
5. **compensation** amount(s); and a
6. **list of cases** in which you have testified as an expert at trial or by deposition within the preceding four years.

> **alignment,**
> **proximity** of items, and **repetition** of boldface

As you will see, the **deadline** for this information is **Sept. 15, 2007.**

If you will submit your statement for reproduction charges, we will reimburse you that same amount. Thank you for assisting us. Please do not hesitate to call me if you require further information.

> subtle, larger type with boldface **contrasts** and emphasizes deadline

Yours truly,

Annabel Garcia
Legal Assistant

Example 3A. Law student resume without proximity or contrast

SIA RAHBARI
909 E. 49th Street
Bloomington, Indiana 47408

home: 333-1393   work: 333-1515

Qualifications

College graduate, first-year law student; flexible, inquisitive; motivated to learn and grow in responsibility and skills; dependable; competent legal research and writing, typing skills; and excellent telephone and people skills.

Skills and Experiences

Organizing — section 1 ambassador to law student council; recruited students into university as Student Ambassador; Teaching Assistant; mentored students; founded International Affairs Club; gathered volunteers, investigated hotel space, transportation, convention rooms for American Freedom Network

Office experience — data entry (membership, donations, shipping orders), answered telephone, delivered messages; Employee Award two months

People skills — bilingual, Spanish; established campus-wide club with variety of majors and backgrounds; Student Ambassador College of Arts

Work Experience

Spring 2001	Office help	Kinko's
Fall, Spring 2002	Teaching Assistant	Political Science
Summer 2000	Enumerator	Federal Bureau of Census
Spring 2000	Fiscal Intern	Indiana Legislature
Summer 1999	Ranch hand, horse trainer	Elsewhere Farms

Education and Training

B.A. with Honors, Indiana University, International Affairs 2002
Indianapolis Community College, 6 hrs (3.4), 1998
Language Arts Academy, Johns High School, Anderson,
Indiana, graduated 1998

no contrasts

no proximity of
headings to
information

alignment
provides no
hierarchy

repetition of
alignment

Example 3B. Law student resume

SIA RAHBARI
909 E. 49th Street
Bloomington, Indiana 47408

home: 333-1395/work: 333-1515

(strong, contrasting type for main categories)

Qualifications

(strong left alignment)

- ▲ Legal research and writing skills, computer skills
- ▲ Legislative, fiscal experience
- ▲ Bilingual (Spanish) public speaker, organizer

(second left alignment for subsections)

Education

- ▲ B.A. Indiana University, with Honors, International Affairs 2006, G.P.A. 3.8
- ▲ Indianapolis Community College, 6 hrs (3.4), 2000
- ▲ Language Arts Academy, Johns High School, Anderson, IN graduated 2000

(g.p.a. slightly larger font, centered)

Work Experience

▲ Teaching Assistant	2004	Indiana University Dept. of Political Science
▲ Fiscal Intern	2002	Indiana Legislature
▲ Enumerator	2002	Federal Bureau of Census
▲ Customer Relations	2003	Kinko's

(all subheads aligned and symbol repeated)

Skills and Experiences

▲ Organizing:	Section 1 Ambassador to law school Student Council
	Indiana University Student Ambassador
	Established campus-wide International Affairs Club
	Scheduled speaking and promotion events
	Investigated space, transportation, convention rooms
▲ Office experience:	Data entry American Freedom Network
	Solicited membership and contributions
	Employee Award two months, Kinko's
▲ People skills:	Taught freshman political science, Indiana University
	Encouraged contributors, American Freedom Network

(repeated alignment)

References

- ▲ Prof. Michael Tigger, Indiana University School of Law, 333-7878
- ▲ Dean Francis Hoole, Indiana University, 333-9882

Example 4A. Law student cover letter

Fredrick Youngdale III
111 Greenberg Drive
Youngdale, Florida 33315
954-874-4598
fyoungd@aol.com

September 16, 2007

Mrs. Hazel Moore
Hiring Partner
Bracewell & Guiliani
1100 Pennzoil Place
Houston, Texas 77002

Dear Mrs. Moore,

Your firm uses second-year law students during the summer. I am applying for that position. I would like to visit your office for an interview when I will be in Houston, Nov. 16-19. Please let me know which day and what time would fit into your busy schedule. I am currently a second-year law student at the University of FarWest Florida. Still, Texas calls. I am currently taking Trial Advocacy and will participate in a mock trial later this fall. As you can tell, I am interested in trial work. Does your firm offer trial experience to summer clerks? These and other questions I hope to have answered in our interview in November. Last summer I worked at my father's firm for six weeks, Youngdale & Youngdale of Miami. I drafted documents and assisted the younger associates as they prepared for big trials. As you can see, I have some legal experience and am eager for more.

Sincerely,

Fredrick Youngdale III

(margin annotations:)
no intitial
information
(RE slot)

weak introduction

one solid
information block

buried skills,
experiences

Example 4B. Law student cover letter

Fredrick Youngdale III
111 Greenberg Drive
Youngdale, Florida 33315
954-874-4598
fyoungd@aol.com

September 16, 2007

Mrs. Hazel Moore
Hiring Partner
Bracewell & Guiliani
1100 Pennzoil Place
Houston, Texas 77002

Re: Summer internship

Dear Mrs. Moore,

Your August advertisement in *Florida Lawyer* caught my interest. Fred
Ledbetter, a second-year associate at Bracewell & Guiliani in Dallas,
recommended that I contact you because your firm focuses on trial work. As
a second-year student at FarWest Florida School of Law, I have a strong,
demonstrated interest in trial work, as evidenced by my participation this
fall in an elective moot court. I would welcome the opportunity to work for
your firm as a summer clerk.

In the course of researching Bracewell & Guiliani, I discovered that your
firm frequently represents clients who are involved in disputes with the
DEA and INS over the seizure of their boats.

- I grew up around boats.
- Last summer I worked on admiralty questions at Youngdale
  & Youngdale as a summer associate.
- This year I am enrolled in Admiralty Law.
- I plan to focus on Admiralty Law when I graduate.

I would like to visit your office for an interview when I will be in Houston,
November 16-19. I hope to meet with you or someone in your office. I will
contact you within the next two weeks and, if possible, arrange a time to
meet that would be convenient. If you prefer, you can contact me at the
number or email address above. Thank you for your consideration.

Sincerely,

Fredrick Youngdale III

Enclosure
Cc: Jack Gershwin, Recruiting Coordinator

Margin notes:

up-front statement
of purpose

introduction
acknowledges where
applicant learned
of job opening

reference to specific
interest

shows interest in
firm — not merely
a form letter

here, **alignment** of
skills and
experience;
repetition of
bullet dots; **contrast**
of list to body
of text;
white space

short paragraphs

Example 5A. Campus sexual harassment policy

SEXUAL HARASSMENT IS AGAINST THE LAW

introduction to underlying law is off-putting to intended audience

no proximity of headings

no contrast for headings

Definitions

"Sexual harassment" — Title VII of the Civil Rights Act of 1964 (employees), Title IX of the Education Amendments of 1972 (students), and University law define sexual harassment as unwelcome sexual advances; requests for sexual favors and other verbal or physical conduct of a sexual nature when submission to such conduct is made a term or condition of one's academic or employment status or is used as a basis for academic or employment decision; or conduct that unreasonably interferes with one's academic pursuits or working conditions by creating a hostile environment.

"*Quid pro quo* harassment" — When a person with authority in the university uses submission to or rejection of unwelcome sexual conduct as the basis for making academic or employment decisions affecting a subordinate, that action is sexual harassment.

"Harasser" — Sexual harassment can occur between supervisors and subordinates, faculty or staff and students, students' peers or co-workers, contractors or visitors and students, or any combination of these.

"Prohibited conduct" — This includes subtle or overt pressure for sexual activity, unnecessary and unwanted touching or brushing against another's body, stalking, sexually suggestive visual displays and/or obscene messages, deliberate assaults or molestations, demands for sexual favors, or promises of preferential treatment or gifts in exchange for sex.

"Unwelcome behavior" — Behavior will be considered unwelcome if the individual did not solicit or invite it and particularly if he or she indicates that the conduct is undesirable or offensive. Acquiescence or failure to complain does not mean that the conduct is welcome. However, if a student or employee actively participates in sexual banter or discussions without giving an indication that the discussion is offensive, it will not be considered unwelcome.

How to report sexual harassment

Report the incident to the dean of students or the equal opportunity officer. Employees, including students who are employed here, who experience sexual harassment in their workplace, should report it to a supervisor or the equal opportunity officer. All complaints and related documents will be maintained in a confidential file and every attempt will be made to ensure the privacy of the individual and the respondent, subject to the university's legal obligations to take necessary disciplinary steps. If it is determined that sexual harassment has occurred, the university will proceed with disciplinary action with or without agreement from the complainant.

Example 5B. Revised sexual harassment policy

SEXUAL HARASSMENT IS AGAINST THE LAW

What is sexual harassment?	What conduct is prohibited?	
		leading questions **contrast** through bold headings
Sexual harassment is	**The law prohibits**	**repetition** of bold tag lines for lists
■ unwelcome sexual advances;	■ subtle or overt pressure for sexual activity;	
■ requests for sexual favors and other verbal or physical conduct of a sexual nature when submission to that conduct is made a term or condition of one's academic or employment status or is used as a basis for academic or employment decision; or	■ unnecessary and unwanted touching or brushing against another's body;	**proximity** of items in list
	■ stalking;	**alignment** of bullet dots
	■ sexually suggestive visual displays and/or obscene messages;	
	■ deliberate assaults or molestations;	
■ conduct that unreasonably interferes with one's academic pursuits or working conditions by creating a hostile environment.	■ demands for sexual favors; or	
	■ promises of preferential treatment or gifts in exchange for sex.	
	Example: You are a work-study student and your boss often puts her arm around you or invites you home after work. You refuse those invitations and dread going to work.	specific action example
Who might be a "harasser"?	**How will someone determine "unwelcome" behavior?**	question format **repeated, aligned**
Sexual harassment can occur between supervisors and subordinates, faculty or staff and students, students, peers or co-workers, contractors or visitors and students, or any combination of these.	Behavior will be considered unwelcome if the individual **did not invite** it and particularly if he or she indicates that the conduct is undesirable or offensive. Failure to complain does not mean that the conduct is welcome.	two main points highlighted with boldface
When **a person with authority** in the university uses submission to or rejection of unwelcome sexual conduct as the basis for making academic or employment decisions affecting a subordinate, that action is "quid pro quo" harassment.	However, if a student or employee actively participates in sexual banter without indicating that the discussion is offensive, it will not be considered unwelcome.	
	Example: You are in an office where many of your male co-workers tell jokes about women and sex. You always break away from the group and change the subject.	**repeated** action example
Title VII of the Civil Rights Act of 1964 (employees), Title IX of the Education Amendments of 1972 (students), and University law.		heavy line detaches source from information

93

What to Remember

- Remember the audience who'll read your document and make it visually inviting: can readers understand what's important through your use of white space and paragraph/sentence length?
- Logically organize both macro and micro levels.
- If the document is important to your future, add the final visual touches of proximity, alignment, repetition, and contrast.
- Read the document one last time to see if it is understandable on the first reading.

CONCLUDING EXERCISES: FORMATTING

Work with the information below and create a **cover letter** for a post-graduate job applying to the medium-sized law firm of Smith & Smith, which has an opening in family law and an opening in litigation. S & S attorney/personnel director Ron Dublanski placed an advertisement in *Illinois Lawyer* announcing two, possibly three, openings for lawyer applicants with no to three years' experience. What skills would you highlight, given Jennifer's goals? What organizational scheme would you use? See possible answers, p. 111.

Jennifer Long
1818 S. Congress Ave.
Chicago, Illinois 60633
773-834-4409
jlong7@aol.com

J.D. University of Chicago expected May 2007, 3.39 g.p.a
Special courses: Trial Advocacy, Children's Rights Clinic
Staff member: Children and the Law Journal; Women and Legal Times Journal

Undergraduate: M.A., Chicago-Kent 2003, Social Work
                 B.A., Chicago-Kent 1997, Social Work
Work: City of Chicago Child Protection Office (investigator),
      1997-1999
      District Attorney's Office, Chicago, paralegal, 2003-2005
Skills: clear prose, interviewing, keeping clear records,
      data spreadsheets, oral argument
Hobbies: Jennifer Lopez memorabilia, hiking
Ref: Prof. Anne Smith, trial advocacy, University of Chicago
       Michael Moore, District Attorney's Office, Chicago
Career goals: I want to practice law in a small family-law firm or with
an agency that specializes in family law. After a few years, I want to do
both trial work and appellate work.

APPENDIX

ANSWERS

CHAPTER 1: REVIEWING THE BASICS

Basic Review #3

1. **correct**. Comma after "Thus" optional.
2. fifty, **four-legged** chairs. Compound adjective before a noun.
3. **here?"** Generally, question marks belong inside quotation marks (see rules 13 and Chapter 5, the punctuation chapter)
4. **assumed**. Assumed = take for granted. Presumed = take upon oneself to dare or go beyond.
5. **barely any**. Double negative.
6. quickly **and** hoped. No single comma between subject (he) and second verb (hoped).
7. **day,** Ed. Comma required at end of beginning adverbial clause.

8. **its**. Possessive pronouns do not have apostrophes (his, her, my, our, their, your, yours).
9. **has no**. No colon after verbs or prepositions.
10. **correct**. Passive voice unnecessary and wordy, but grammatically correct.

Basic Review #4

1. everyone **was** determined to research **his**. Singular pronoun "everyone" requires singular verb and possessive pronoun.
2. **different from**. Incorrect usage.
3. two errors: **saying,** "Your; . . . and commas." Commas required before quoted material that doesn't complete the textual sentences. Plus, commas and periods belong inside quotation marks.
4. **because** he. Traditionally, because = causality, and since = time.
5. librarian**,** who had been a paralegal in his earlier life**,** explained. Commas around a non-essential clause.
6. **correct**. In context the pronoun is identifiable, but you may choose to replace "his" with "Ed's."
7. **Ed hoped** the list would. "Hopefully" means only "with hope" and modifies "list."
8. to find **only whether**. Misplaced modifier.
9. law **that** he needed. Essential clause (unless what's important is only the specific law, and not his need for it).
10. could **infer**. Infer = suggest a connection. Imply = hint at something.

Basic Review #5

1. for inmates and **him**. Object of preposition "for."
2. three errors:
   a. metal chairs, he. Punctuation of introductory phrase.
   b. if there **were**. Subjunctive mood when a wish or contrary to fact.
   c. ineffective-counsel cases. Compound adjectives describing "cases."

3. had **slowed.** Incorrect verb form.

4. **drawer and** removed. No single comma between subject and second verb. Optional: comma after "reluctantly."

5. top **that** had. Essential, restrictive phrase (rather important to Ed) requires "that" and no comma.

6. to **him.** "Himself" is reflexive.

7. law; however, he; law. **H**owever, he. Two independent sentences require terminal punctuation.

8. Canon 6: "A lawyer."

9. to **ensure.** Ensure = make something certain. Insure = with money, guarantees. Assure = remove doubt from someone's mind.

10. **correct.** Good luck, Ed!

CHAPTER 2: ORGANIZATION

Concluding Exercises

1. **Organization.** Begin with a conclusion.

We agree with Rentacar. Rentacar argues that Louisiana should not adopt the dangerous instrumentality theory in the context of automobile liability. The McPhails contend that Louisiana should recognize automobiles as dangerous instrumentalities and hold commercial owners/renters liable when their vehicles are negligently operated, but have no law to support their stance. Instead, they claim that public policy considerations support their contention. Louisiana has not passed such a law, and we will not create that policy here.

2. **Thesis and road maps.** Thesis/conclusion first. Rule. Facts. Conclusion.

Powe should probably not be sanctioned for a Rule 11 violation. Rule 11 of the Federal Rules of Civil Procedure requires attorneys to certify that any pleading or written motion is filed not to harass, or to delay, and to certify that the claims and contentions are not frivolous. In this case, Powe believed that his motion on behalf of the teacher was backed by strong evidence that she had been discriminated against by her administration. He had no knowledge of a Fourth Circuit requirement that a client must go through collective bargaining as a member of a school district. Thus he counseled her not to ask for collective bargaining before the filing. Because the facts show that Powe did not file to harass, delay, or present frivolous motions, he should not be sanctioned.

3. Headings.

    a. Rule 11 is intended to prevent frivolous filings.
    b. Powe had evidence of discrimination.
    c. A Fourth Circuit requirement for collective bargaining does not present an issue of frivolous filings.

4. Road map paragraphs and headings. The headings are **not** anticipated and thus not effective. Replace with something like this:

    a. Federal courts generally accept attorney evidence of good faith.
    b. Federal courts are split on requiring collective bargaining.

5. Headings. No, they do not follow the setup.

    a. The court will find Grimes's procedural errors to be negligence.
    b. An investigation of the client contract will reveal whether Grimes breached the contract.
    c. The court will probably reject any DTPA claims because Grimes did not knowingly misfile or misrepresent his client.

6. Headings should follow the setup.

a. The Sixth Amendment requires effective assistance.
b. Case law requires thorough research.
c. Rule of Appellate Procedure 38.1 provides guidelines for brief form.

7. This paragraph is incomplete without its thesis.

> • • • • • •
>
> **C.** The Oregon Supreme Court does not recognize an exception for lawyer dishonesty.
>
> The Oregon Supreme Court, in the recent *In re Gatti*, 8 P.3d 966 (Or. 2000), sanctioned a lawyer who misrepresented his identity while attempting to investigate a claim of insurance fraud. Thus, the Oregon court refused to recognize "an exception for any lawyer to engage in dishonesty." 8 P.3d at 976. Not all states adopt as strict an approach. New York, for example, has long recognized prosecutorial exceptions to the dishonesty rule.

8. Transitions.

The court agrees with the plaintiff. **First**, determinations under Federal Rules of Evidence 104(b) must be based upon admissible evidence. Fed. R. Evid. 104(b) at 1230. **Next**, Rule 104(b) applies only to determinations of "the relevancy of evidence." **Since** determining whether a document is a business record does not involve the document's relevancy, we conclude that Rule 104(b) does not apply.

Finally, the court itself should determine whether a document is within Rule 803(b). In no known instance has the question of the legitimacy of a 803(b) status business record been a matter for the jury. The Third Circuit agreed with this reasoning in *In re Japanese Electronics Products*, 723 F.2d 238, 287-88 (3d Cir. 1983).

9. Topic sentences and transitions.

Attorneys have a duty of reasonable care to serve their clients. **For example**, in 1989 the Texas Supreme Court found, in Walder v. Texas, 85 S.W.3d 824, 829 (2002), that counsel must serve a client to the best of his or her ability. **In Walder**, counsel did not identify the appropriate standard for appellate review of a revocation order. **More recently**, in 2002, the same court held that counsel had a duty to act as a reasonably prudent professional. Cosgrove v. Grimes, 774 S.W.2d 662 (Tex. 1989). **There**, counsel did not recognize the statute of limitations in a car accident that occurred in another state. Gerardi's issue is whether an attorney's overlooking a major development in case law violates the standard of reasonable care.

10. Transitions.

Pamela Hunter **filed a class-action suit** on behalf of a group of North Carolina bakery workers. **These workers** believed that their **company-owned** bakery had violated Title VII of the Civil Rights Act of 1964 when the **owners** closed **this bakery** but not others. **The owners** had publicly stated that **this particular bakery** would remain open throughout the year.

Ms. Hunter **alleged** that the bakery had a pattern and practice of racial discrimination. Compared to the predominately white workers at **other company-owned bakeries**, the predominately African-American workers in this bakery were more skilled but paid less. The bakery denied the **allegations** and **furthermore** insisted that any Title VII claims had to be arbitrated under a collective bargaining agreement (**CBA**).

The bakery **then** argued that Hunter knew, or should have known, of the **CBA** and asked the court to impose a Rule 11 sanction on Hunter for filing a lawsuit before arbitration. The North Carolina court sanctioned her and suspended her legal practice for five years **although** five other circuits have held that Title VII claims do not have to be first arbitrated under a CBA.

CHAPTER 3: SENTENCES

Exercise 1: Unraveling Tough Sentences

1. The district **court noted** (1) that the report was *Brady* material because the report did identify the fraud procurement advisor as a favorable witness, and (2) that the advisor might have testified that the government did not suffer any economic loss when the scholars plagiarized. The **court then concluded** that the material should have been disclosed.

2. On those factual grounds, the court concluded **that** the report does contain exculpatory material, **that** the government failed to respond to the defendant's specific requests for the material, and **that** there is a reasonable probability that testimony from Kennedy could have influenced the trial. **Therefore,** the report should have been disclosed by the government as *Brady* material.

3a. The advisor felt morally bound to report the questionable behavior to the university's honor committee because a roommate of one of the Ph.D. students discussed the issue with her own advisor and that faculty member had been worried about government funding of academic projects.

3b. A roommate of one of the Ph.D. students discussed the issue with her own advisor. That faculty member had been worried about government funding of academic projects, and therefore she felt morally bound to report the questionable behavior to the university's honor committee.

4a. The **prosecution violates** due process when it suppresses requested evidence favorable to an accused if the evidence is material either to guilt or punishment, irrespective of the good or bad faith of the prosecution.

4b. The **prosecution violates** due process when it suppresses requested evidence favorable to an accused when the evidence is material either to guilt or punishment. **Due process is violated** irrespective of the good or bad faith of the prosecution.

5. A third-year law **student plagiarized** a nationally syndicated columnist in a law student newsletter.

6. A member of the **Federalist Society uncovered** the original column.

7. **Administrators** later **learned** that the **student meant** to edit the column before he published it.

Exercise 2: Avoiding Errors

1. [As written, "who" modifies graduate students] One student tried at least twice to notify the titular head of all graduate students, the **Dean, who** she thought would understand her situation.

2. After researching both primary and secondary sources, you must turn in a draft **four weeks before graduation** and have it read and edited within two weeks of graduation.

3. This court reversed **only** the convictions for "degrees for contracts" but allowed the defendants to renew their Rule 14 claims in district court.

4. The court questioned whether the government investigation included information material to the plaintiffs' facts and if **this undisclosed information** would thus establish a legitimate *Brady* claim.

5. The plaintiffs had their understanding of the material but the government kept the some of material from the plaintiff's lawyer, so it was up to the court to review **all of the material**.

6. Ph.D. candidates are expected to do their own research and write their own original papers. Newspapers wrote a series of articles about **these particular candidates**.

7. Who is "he," "his," or "him"?

8. Within a graduate department, the faculty is always divided over **how many** graduate students one faculty member can supervise simultaneously and **how many** students the faculty member should teach without appropriate help from teaching assistants.

9. In defense of dissertation, a student must present
   a. an oral defense of the topic's thesis;
   b. **an original thesis that is not** a repetition of another's earlier work;

c. a bibliography of works consulted; and

d. proof of a supervisor's work with drafts and alternative hypotheses.

10. A Ph.D. candidate must ask his chairman for direction, sources, **and** personal library holding, **and the candidate** must give him or her the draft early enough for feedback.

Exercise 3. Incorporating Authority

1. The **Sixth Circuit** originally set forth facts of the plagiarism case against the plaintiffs in this action. <u>United States v. Frost</u>, 125 F.3d 346 (6th Cir. 1997).

2. After the Supreme Court decided, in <u>Brady v. Maryland</u>, 373 U.S. 83 (1963), that suppression by prosecutors of evidence favorable to the accused violates due process, **the Court later reviewed** the materiality requirement and said a "touchstone of materiality is a reasonable probability of a different result." <u>Kyles v. Whitley</u>, 514 U.S. 419 (1995).

3. The **Mail Fraud Act prohibits** people from scheming to defraud the United States of money or property. 18 U.S.C. §1341.

Concluding Exercises

1a. **[front loaded] Defendant Bite was** owner and president of FIG, a private atmospheric-research firm that relied primarily on contracts with government agencies including NASA and the Department of Defense, **and he was also** a professor at the University of Tennessee Space Institute (UTSI).

1b. Professor Bite has impressive credentials: **(1)** owner and president of FIG, a private atmospheric-research firm that relied primarily on contracts with government agencies including NASA and the Department of Defense, **and (2)** a professor at the University of Tennessee Space Institute (UTSI).

2. **[passive, ambiguous "they"] Plaintiffs decided** to bifurcate their claims and to split into their individual cases so that the court could hear

both the claims and the individuals separately and perhaps more fairly.

3. **[repeated "that," thus not parallel]** The students may have thought **that,** as long as the supervising professor knew of and approved their use of outside materials, they were adequately documenting their material.

4. **[long sentence]** An attorney or unrepresented party, by presenting a pleading, motion, or other paper to the court, is certifying that he/she has a proper purpose. **The** attorney thus certifies that the filing is not being presented for any improper purpose. **The** attorney **is also** certifying that other legal contentions in the document are warranted by existing law and other allegations and factual contentions have evidentiary support or are likely to have evidentiary support after a reasonable opportunity for further investigation or discovery. **Finally, the** attorney certifies that the denials of factual contentions are warranted on the evidence, or are reasonably based on a lack of information or belief.

5. **[lack of parallelism]** The grand jury returned thirty-one indictments against multiple defendants, charging them **with scheming** to defraud the United States of money or property and **with aiding and abetting in the** in obstruction of justice.

6. **[misplaced word]** Ph.D. students may include material in their written work **only** if they acknowledge the primary sources and keep the material exactly as it was originally.

7. **[back-to-back citations]** In an unpublished opinion, the Sixth Circuit had complicated original facts and a tangled time line, referred to in United States v. Potter, 234 F.3d 1270 (6th Cir. 2000). **Earlier the same court** had looked at the same facts, so the court could rely on their earlier decision for help through the lengthy list of names and causes. United States v. Frost, 125 F.3d 346 (6th Cir. 1997).

8. **[ambiguous, truncated passive]** The **defendants filed** motions for acquittals, and the **court rendered** a decision only days later.

9. **[ambiguous pronoun]** He had just faced his first interview with the hysterical adult daughter of a woman who'd been bludgeoned to death by [**the daughter's/the mother's**] drunken husband.

10. [dangling element] Believing that unpleasant secrets from the ivory-tower university were to be revealed, **townspeople** packed the courtroom hoping to hear what made academics so different from ordinary citizens.

CHAPTER 4: WORDS

Concluding Exercises

1. to evaluate
2. The judge **said** that he had never seen such a blatant use of another's work.
3. Fender was obliged legally and probably morally as well.
4. Fred Fender refuted this charge and contended also that he has been unfairly persecuted into a morass that his secretary was responsible for. (concluding preposition acceptable, but you can change it)
5. Fender pointed to various defenses, to wit: the pressure of time, his inexperienced secretarial pool, the length of the ACLU filing.
6. postage-guaranteed envelopes
7. deeply frightened secretary (CORRECT because -ly signals an adverb.)
8. clerk's new, heightened awareness *or* newly heightened
9. well established code of conduct (CORRECT because "well" is already a correctly used adverb)
10. big-firm CLE compliance
11. To thoroughly **investigate** the two, similar filings, the clerk **necessarily** worked late.
12. The next morning the clerk **presented** proof to the judge that **reinforced** the ACLU's research.
13. Fender's new **resolve** to do his own work merely **continued** a lifetime of living on the edge.
14. It was ~~very~~ unique for an attorney to address the court and the public about his error. ("unique" cannot be modified)
15. Fender thanked the court for allowing him to **publicly present** his new-found, original writing skills in a CLE class.

16. When the judge found the clerk in the office at 7:30 a.m., he worried that the clerk was there too early.

17. This type ~~and kind~~ of dishonesty reflected on the ~~truth and~~ veracity of any big-time lawyer and on the court.

18. The attorney **was probably obligated** whether or not the document was an official court filing. [to replace the "or not" here would either create ambiguity or take additional words]

19. **[modifiers ending in–ly are already adverbs and do not need hyphens]** The overly confident law firm had no document-review system to catch this problem.

20. **["which" is ambiguous]** ~~It is important to note that~~ the signature at the bottom of a legal document means the attorney legally accepts ~~is a legal an acceptance by the attorney of~~ professional responsibility for the writing, and the secretary cannot be held responsible for its content. ~~which~~ **This convention** is consistent with our understanding of all professional documents.

21. **[misplaced modifier]** When an attorney works **only for** himself, he has no one else to blame for errors.

22. **[dangling]** After researching for any other similar cases, **the judge** discovered ~~there appear to be~~ several instances of plagiarism that other jurisdictions dealt with publicly.

23. **[ambiguous "this"]** The judge found for the ACLU and ordered a strict scrutiny of all of Fender's firm's documents. **This decision** was followed by a public announcement.

24. **[wordy]** ~~Let us just say that~~ this firm will also penalize Mr. Fender and will not allow this sloppy writing to be duplicated ~~in the future~~.

25. because

26. discreet

27. its

28. ensure

29. infer

30. continual

31. In this case, the judge knew he had to decide based on his own ethics.

32. Normally, a judge does not have to begin a day with a sanction.

33. The judge considered a number of punishments, **e.g.,** CLE classes, a two-month bar from his court, a close scrutiny of every document that firm filed, **etc.**

CHAPTER 5: PUNCTUATION

Concluding Exercises

1. In Dallas **[optional comma]** a 16-year-old kid **[compound adjective]** with a decidedly **[-ly no hyphen]** red convertible was stopped for speeding.

2. He pulled over to the side of the road **[one independent clause] and** was so nervous he hit the curb.

3. "Ohmygod no," the policeman heard him chanting. **[comma within quotation marks]**

4. "This will be an easy stop," the policeman said into his car speaker, **[dependent clause follows]** "because he is already admitting he's in trouble."

5. First **[optional comma]** he walked completely around the car, noting its condition; **[list with internal commas so semicolons are required to separate the three verb modules]** stopped by the passenger window; **[punctuation before "and" in a series]** and asked to see the boy's driver's license.

6. He asked for information: **[colon, not dash, before a list]** the driver's name, the owner of the vehicle, the driver's destination, and the driver's knowledge of the speed limit.

7. The police officer said, **[no indent for short quotations]** "You have the right to not answer these simple questions, but I advise you to."

8. When the boy quickly spouted the answers, **[comma after introductory clause]** the police officer wrote several of them down **[no comma between noun and its second verb]** and grunted at the rest.

9. The process needed to go quickly, **[comma for nonessential clause]** which the officer knew from experience.

10. Some speeders will become indignant and argumentative, **[comma between two independent clauses with a conjunction]** and some will be embarrassed and just want to sign the forms and leave.

CHAPTER 6: FORMAT

Concluding Exercise

1818 S. Congress Avenue
Chicago, Illinois 60633
773-834-4409
jlong7@aol.com
April 15, 2007

Smith & Smith
1717 Centerpoint
Chicago, Illinois 60633

identify job opening

Re: Attorney Employment

Dear Mr. Dublanski,

express specific interest

I saw your advertisement in Illinois Lawyer and am applying for a position as family law attorney. My skills and my goals make me a good match for this job.

law education background that matches opening

I am graduating from the University of Chicago Law School with a special concentration in family law and litigation. I took both the Children's Rights Clinic and Trial Advocacy, and spent most of my free time helping the clinic with family-law issues.

work experience that matches opening

My work experience also parallels the Smith & Smith job: I was an investigator for three years with the City of Chicago Child Protection Office. Just before law school, I worked for a year as a paralegal in the Chicago District Attorney's Office, where I handled cases and issues in family law on a daily basis. My B.A. and M.A. in Social Work from Chicago-Kent gave me the theoretical framework for both jobs, and now my

educational background

legal education has developed my understanding of the law behind the cases and personalities I encountered.

link to city

I am interested in both family law and litigation and plan to practice in the Chicago area. I would very much appreciate an opportunity to discuss your current openings.

professional tone

Sincerely,

Jennifer Long

leaves details to resume

enclosure: resume

INDEX